Foreword by

HARRISON E. SALISBURY

The 900 Days: The Siege of Leningrad

Translated, edited, and with an afterword by

NORMAN LUXENBURG

Feffer & Simons, Inc.
London and Amsterdam

SIEGE and
SURVIVAL

*The Odyssey
of a Leningrader*

ELENA SKRJABINA

Southern Illinois University Press

Carbondale and Edwardsville

Copyright © 1971 by Southern Illinois University Press
All rights reserved
Printed in the United States of America
Designed by Andor Braun
International Standard Book Number 0–8093–0511–9
Library of Congress Catalog Card Number 70–156790

Contents

Foreword

When the 900-day siege of Leningrad was finally lifted and the gaunt, brave survivors had basked a bit in the fitful spring sunshine, the Soviet government made one of its rare graceful gestures to these heroic people. It awarded to the survivors (and to some who did not) the Medal for Defense of Leningrad.

So far as I know it played no favorites in this. Those who had chanced to come through alive got the medal (many of them to their great surprise). In all more than 300,000 medals were passed out—and it may sound like a very large total. But when you consider the fact that something like 3,300,000 persons were trapped within the siege lines when the long blockade began on September 8, 1941, the number is not so large. Of course, between 1,100,000 and 1,500,000 persons died during the siege—of hunger, of cold, of disease, of German bullets, bombs, and shells.

The Leningrad medal does not seem to have been awarded to Leningraders who spent the terrifying months of November and December 1941, and the incredible January, February, and March of 1942 in the city but who were toward the end of that period evacuated at enormous peril and under such hardships that tens of thousands froze to death or died of other causes in the perilous crossing of Lake Ladoga or in the disorganized, ill-equipped facilities which were provided for the outward migrants on the far shore of Lake Ladoga or in the freezing and starving countryside around the railhead, leading back to the "mainland" of Russia which so many had expected to be their salvation.

The perils and trials of the exodus from Leningrad —the assembly in the dying city on a windswept corner with nothing but ice, snow, and the quickly covered frozen corpses of the Leningraders to mark the landscape; the journey in unheated trucks or jammed into jerky trains which often took twenty-four hours to make a run of about twenty-two miles; the wait on the Arctic shores of Ladoga for the crossing; the ordeal of the ice, often marked by break-downs (quickly resulting in death by cold), strafing by low-flying Nazi planes, accidents which pitched the refugees into bomb-torn holes in the ice and certain death; the failure to provide any place for the evacuees to sleep, eat, or warm themselves when they reached the far shores—all of these, and many other tests of human fortitude, the Leningraders went through. For these there was no reward. Not even a medal. If they managed to preserve their life and that of any of their loved ones, that was sufficient.

All of this Elena Skrjabina has experienced. She has no Medal of Leningrad. But she possesses a distinction which is as rare as any human being possesses. She *is* a Leningrader. She endured the siege. She came out over Lake Ladoga—not alone. She brought her mother, two children and an old nurse with her. She did not emerge without loss; her mother died. Her mother survived the bitter days of siege. She even lived through December

1941, and January 1942, into February 1942. She survived the trip across the ice. But once on the other side, her strength was gone. She endured a few days in the hospital. Not more. Then she slipped away from life as hundreds of thousands of her fellow Leningraders had before her. Madame Skrjabina with the tenacity, the same courage, and the stubbornness which the Red Army displayed in fighting against such terrible odds against the Nazis, survived that catastrophe. She almost lost one of her sons. He was so near death that she had to leave him in a primitive hospital. Then, she herself and the younger boy were near their last dregs of strength when by a quirk of fate stranger than a novel's, the family was reunited in a twinkling and, together, on a wonderfully warm, well-provisioned, comfortable hospital train, was carried southward and eastward out of the paths of danger to a safe refuge far behind the Russian lines.

The fact that their ultimate refuge in the Caucasus by an equally strange fate was overrun by the Nazis and that this opened a new odyssey in the life of Madame Skrjabina is another story—one which she tells in dramatic terms. It was this second ordeal which finally had a happy ending—the casting up upon American shores of Madame Skrjabina where since she has made a new life in Russian studies at the University of Iowa.

In writing my work on Leningrad, *The 900 Days: the Siege of Leningrad*, I sought to tell the epic in so far as was humanly possible in the words of the Leningraders themselves. I talked to survivors in Leningrad. I read their letters, their reminiscences, studied their diaries. I found that by no means all of the survivors were in Leningrad. Some, like Mad-

ame Skrjabina, were in the United States. Others
were in Paris. Others in South America. And, of
course, even in the Soviet Union, not all the Leningraders returned to their great city. Wherever I
met these people I felt instantly I was in the presence
of a different race, a different breed. I finally got so
that I could almost invariably recognize a Leningrader in Russia even without being told. These
were people who held their heads a bit higher. Who
walked a bit straighter. Whose very presence told
you that they were not ordinary. Indeed, they were
not. They were people who had endured so much
they could never be frightened of anything again. I
like to think that even when the Leningrad city
leaders were, incredibly, being executed by Stalin's
police on the insane charges that they had proposed
to deliver the city to the enemy, they went before
the execution squad with upraised heads and eyes
that dared the cowardly gunmen to do with their
bullets what Nazi guns, what 40-below cold, what
starvation, darkness, ice, and gloom had been unable to do.

The best way to *feel* the Leningrad epic is to read
it in one of the diaries and that of Madame Skrjabina
is outstanding in this regard. She was an ordinary
woman living an ordinary life with an ordinary
family and ordinary friends on June 22, 1941. Suddenly the whole world changed. We read in the
entries on her pages how the walls begin to close in,
how the spirit of the people began to be buffeted,
the trials, the fears, the dangers, the divisions (for
not all the Leningraders were brave and heroic),
the rumors, and then, finally, the bitter, appalling
truth—the city had been cut off. It was without connection with the rest of Russia. The food stores had

been burned in the terrible Nazi air raid on the Badaev warehouses. No need to retell the whole story here. Better to read it in the simple, eloquent words of Madame Skrjabina. She *lived* it. And that is why she needs no Medal to wear on her chest. No more than any Leningrader does. You can see that golden spark in her eyes just as you can see it in all of those who endured. It is a light that never died. To be in the presence of a Leningrader is in itself an honor, and we share a little of that light, reflected from the pages of her book.

Harrison E. Salisbury

New York City
January 1971

Leningrad

June 22, 1941 to February 6, 1942

JUNE 22

This morning everything was as peaceful and calm as a still lake. The sun was shining and everything seemed to promise a perfect day. I was preparing to go to Pushkin with my friend, Irina Levitskaya, to visit a sick boy, bedridden with tuberculosis. My elder son, Dima, with his inseparable friend Sergei, was getting ready for a long-awaited excursion to Peterhof. The boys had never been there and they were especially excited because today marked the opening of the Peterhof fountains.

The fresh morning air, the sunshine streaming through the wide-open windows and the fact that everything seemed to be going so well combined to give me a wonderful feeling of contentment and joy. Outside the door of my bedroom I could hear the whisperings of our nana, the nurse, as she tried to restrain my five-year-old son, Yura, who was anxious, as usual, to awaken me. After breakfast, I hurriedly finished some urgent typing so I could be free to leave for Pushkin on time.

At around nine o'clock, the phone rang. It was my husband calling from work. Though usually calm, he seemed greatly agitated. Without explain-

3

ing why, he asked me not to go anywhere and to keep Dima at home. But Dima had already left. My husband's warnings gave rise to a vague anxiety, but the likelihood of any disaster was certainly far from my mind.

At noon my mother and I heard Molotov speak on the radio. So this was it—war! Germany was already bombing Soviet cities. Molotov's speech was halting, as if he were out of breath. His rallying, spirited appeals seemed out of place. And suddenly I realized that something ominous and oppressive loomed over us.

After the broadcast I ran out into the street. The city was in confusion and uproar. People were hastily exchanging word, filling the stores, buying up everything they could lay their hands on, aimlessly milling about the streets. Many rushed to the bank to withdraw their savings. This panic seized me. I, too, hurried to withdraw those rubles listed in my bank book. But I was too late. The bank had run out of money. The payments had stopped. People clamored, demanding. The June day blazed on with unbearable heat. Someone fainted. Someone else swore vehemently. Not until evening did everything become somehow strangely still. Like the quiet before an autumn storm.

JUNE 23

I spent a sleepless night. In bed early, at eleven, I could not get to sleep. My nerves were much too tense. Too many disquieting thoughts keep entering my mind. What will become of us? My husband called again in the evening and said he could not be home because he had been put on duty at the factory.

This was especially unpleasant at such an anxious time. I had barely fallen asleep at about two in the morning when suddenly I was aroused by deafening gunfire. I couldn't understand what was happening. It seemed Leningrad was already being bombed and that everything around us would crumble. Our family and the other tenants gathered in the vestibule, considering it the safest place to be. There were no windows and so the shooting outside sounded muffled.

Our neighbor Lubov Nikolayevna Kurakina was orating above the din. Her husband, a former party member, had already served two years on a charge of counterrevolution. Although her Communist sympathies had been shaken after the arrest of her husband, this night under the roar of the antiaircraft guns, she forgot all her previous resentment. With conviction she extolled the invincibility of Soviet Russia. To some degree, her conviction was calming and reassuring, but it was impossible to alleviate completely our alarm.

Anastasia Vladimirovna, our former landlady, was sitting on a tall trunk and smiling sarcastically. She made no attempt to hide her hatred for the Soviet government and saw in this war and the eventual victory of the Germans the only possible salvation. In many respects, I share her views; but that smile irritates me. Two sentiments entered the controversy; the wish to believe that Russia would not be destroyed and the realization that only war affords any actual possibility to be free of the terror of the regime.

The antiaircraft guns fired for three hours. There are many of them placed in Leningrad proper and its vicinity. Toward morning everything plunged back into silence.

5

JUNE 23, *evening*

The day passed comparatively quietly. My husband came home tired after night duty. He tried to cheer us up, to raise our spirits. I went to the ticket office of the Alexander Theatre to return tickets bought two weeks ago for *A Nest of Gentlefolk*, a play based on the novel by Turgenev. I had very much wanted to see this performance which was highly praised by everyone, but the prospect of sitting inside the theater waiting for a repetition of last night's bombing destroyed that wish.

JUNE 24

Today brought the beginning of the "great resettlement of the people." The Tarnovski family came to us. Their own apartment is near the Putilovski Plant and they are afraid this industrial sector will be among the first to be bombed. So we made room for them. We gave one of our four rooms to the young Tarnovskis, George and his wife, and settled his mother on the couch in my room. It is crowded even by our Soviet standards. My mother grumbles, but I am satisfied. There is quite a bit of truth to the saying, "Company in distress makes trouble less."

JUNE 25

Now our family is seldom together. It is only the fourth day of war and the normal, everyday routine has been upset. Our windows are blacked out. Thick, blue paper blinds separate us from the familiar city, from the street which passes by the walls of our house. Simultaneously with this isolation from the outside world appears the pressing need to concentrate all one's interests in those nearest him, in one's relatives, in one's family.

The younger children, Yura and his friend Vitya, play war games all day long. Only neither one wants to be a German. Our nana is entrusted with this role. As a result she always suffers defeat and the boys fill the house with shouts of conquest. They still do not realize the seriousness of our situation. It is another matter with Dima. He listens to all the radio announcements, confers with his friends at school and brings all the news to us.

It is quiet. The antiaircraft guns are silent. I must take advantage of the silence and am writing this now that the boys are asleep.

JUNE 26

Late last night I had a great shock. I was already in bed when our neighbor Lubov Nikolayevna burst in with a cry, "Hide Yura! Quickly!"

Hurriedly she told me the latest news. The order had been given to evacuate all children from Leningrad. Mothers are not allowed to accompany them. The children will be sent to Bologoye, Staraya Russa, and other designated towns. But it is just as dangerous. The Germans are advancing with unbelievable speed and are bombing everywhere. I became so frightened that there could not even have been any thought of sleep. My heart thumped and my thoughts became confused. I didn't know what to do or what to decide. The idea of separating from Yura is so horrible to me that I am ready to do anything to keep him. I have decided to defy the order. I won't give up my son for anything. For the rest of the night I tossed and turned, falling asleep for minutes at a time. Nightmares tormented me. Yura—torn from my arms. I pull him back, back to me until at last my strength fails me, and I can struggle no longer.

JUNE 27

At one A.M. there was a piercing bell, the kind that stops the heart. Anyone who lives in the Soviet Union knows what the purpose of such an especially long night bell is. This is the sound that means a search warrant or an order for arrest. But this time it turned out to be a summons from the Draft Board. We had been expecting this. Although my husband had not been called up during the Finnish War, this time the situation is quite different.

JUNE 28

Today is Saturday, a day of great tumult. It all began with a phone call from my friend, Kholmyanskaya, the wife of the technical director of the factory where my husband works. She proposes that I leave with the so-called "factory kindergarten" to take the children in the direction of Moscow. There it would be possible for us to live and work with this kindergarten. Kholmyanskaya further said that she is going along with her child and tried to persuade me not to hesitate any longer, but to join right away. In her opinion, this is the only way Dima, Yura, and I can stay together. Besides that, she is certain that hard times lie ahead for Leningrad.

I went to the factory. The director repeated Kholmyanskaya's words and included me in the group of "governesses." At first glance everything seems to be working out well. At the same time, I am faced with a serious problem. And that is, that although I could take Dima and Yura with me, I would have to leave my mother and our elderly nana behind. When I returned home with this news, my mother burst into tears. She is terrified that in such a way we might part forever. Nana is overcome and silent. I am literally between two fires. On one hand, I understand perfectly well that the children must be saved, and on the other hand, I pity these helpless women. How can I leave them to the mercy of fate?

I cannot believe that there can be a famine in Leningrad. We are constantly being told of the plentiful food supplies which, supposedly, could last us many years. And as for the threat of bombings—we are also constantly assured of the capabilities of our high-power antiaircraft defense system and that Leningrad couldn't possibly be subjected to shelling. If this is even half true, then why try to leave?

JUNE 29

My cousin Marina dropped in. She is terrified by the war. She would run heedlessly wherever she could. At first she wanted to send her ten-year-old son away with his school. Later it turned out that the Hermitage, where she works, is being evacuated and that she will be allowed to take her boy with her. She calls my reluctance to leave with the factory kindergarten "madness." As a result of all these conversations, arguments, and advice, I packed a few things and prepared some food. I am waiting to see what develops.

My mother and nana, who yesterday had been so overwhelmed by the possibility of my leaving with the children, today decided to sacrifice themselves.

They are trying to convince me that it is my duty to evacuate and save the children.

But it was not for me to decide after all. The telephone rang. Between sobs, Kholmyanskaya informed me that all the plans had fallen through. The workers revolted and nearly tore the factory committee apart when they learned the factory planned to send off its so-called intelligentsia, so to speak, with the kindergarten. The trip will not take place. I could not hide my joy; my agonizing problem has been resolved by this circumstance. It no longer depends on me. I no longer have to worry about abandoning my mother and nana. There will be no parting.

JUNE 30

However, they are still evacuating the children in earnest. Almost all of my acquaintances are sending away their small children and adolescents. Marina has left with her Oleg for Yaroslav province. My neighbor Lubov Nikolayevna rushed to Byelorussiya where her children have been for two months with her maid's family. When will she get there?

Her face still wet with tears, my close friend Elizaveta Sergeyevna was dressing her three-year-old daughter for evacuation. Her parents and husband barely convinced her to make this decisive step. It is terrible to part at such moments.

The antiaircraft artillery is quiet. Could it really be that air raids do not threaten Leningrad?

JULY 1

I am shaken by terrible news. My friend and co-worker Byelskaya was arrested. Why? Another one of the many puzzles. Of course no one will explain anything. They came at night, searched, found nothing, confiscated nothing, but took her away anyway. All I know is that the head of the institute where we both work is very hostile toward her. It could be that the charge is "foreign ties." I am greatly concerned for her. Moreover, I know her family situation: her brother, drafted, a tubercular sister, an aging mother, and a three-year-old daughter. I went to see them and spent nearly half an hour. At my home, they had all decided that I, too, had been arrested.

JULY 4

The troubles in Leningrad brought me to an unexpected decision. To go away from these troubles. Therefore, I went to Tyarlevo and rented a cottage. This year the cottages are vacant. Pick what you want. Ordinarily I would never have done this. The prices there are generally very high. But the picture is different now. All the cottages stand empty.

JULY 5

Airplanes do fly this far and the majority of them are German. Sometimes there are even air battles. People have not yet fully realized what war is. They are reckless. Instead of hiding in their basements during air raids, they pour out into the streets. This air of security has worked its spell. We, too, disregard the danger and watch the battles as if they were a spectacular show.

The news in the papers grows more and more alarming. Towns, one after another, are being taken by the Germans. Trains rattle by, carrying women and youths mobilized to dig trenches. My husband is staying in Leningrad. As he was called into active duty there, he was ordered to take necessary military training.

JULY 8

Every week I have to go into Leningrad to check the apartment and to visit my husband at his barracks. I am writing this, having returned from Leningrad. I visited my husband and then stopped by the apartment. Nothing has changed. Everything is still as bleak as ever. People continue to rush about. Everyone seems to think that the sector in which he lives is the most dangerous one, that he would be safer with friends. My uncle and aunt moved to our apartment, all because our place seems more secure. They have taken over Yura's room. Of course I let them. Right now, we are not living in the city and if we should return, the last thing we would think of is comfort.

Every day there is new disquieting news. First they warn us that the Germans will certainly use gas (the one thing that frightens me most) and then there are rumors that Leningrad will be taken within a month. More often the talk is about the inevitable famine because all those newspaper assurances of our massive food supplies are barefaced lies.

People are being sent away by the thousands and by the tens of thousands to dig trenches. All institutions have been converted into mobilizing places. Those employees who do go to work are generally organized into brigades and then sent off to the front lines. No one is excused—young girls in sundresses and sandals, young boys in shorts and sportshirts. They are not even allowed to go home to change clothes. Of how much use can they really be? City youths do not even know how to use a shovel, much less those heavy crowbars they must use to break up the dry, clay soil. Conditions at the trenches are extreme. The workers must sleep wherever they can, often under the open sky. As a result, many catch a chill, get sick, but absolutely no one is excused from duty.

Young Tarnovskaya, who lives with us, is among the victims. I found her in bed with a high fever. Yesterday, when she returned from her place of work, it turned out that except for a light sundress, she had very little protective outer clothing on. Apparently she will be ill for a long time.

Kurakin, the husband of my next door neighbor Lubov Nikolayevna came back home from the concentration camp yesterday. For two years she petitioned and beat down doors to get a review of his case to no avail. The war has helped. They have released him. At first, Lubov was in seventh heaven. She couldn't believe he was back. Now that the initial ardor has passed, a strained, strange relationship has grown up between them. He is fearful, crushed, jumpy, afraid to speak. In a whisper, she tells me what he endured. She tells me that they beat him cruelly and often, demanding some sort of confession of his "crimes." He has a broken rib and is deaf in one ear.

Lubov tells of her own adventures. She has just returned from Byelorussiya where she went to find her children. She walked right into hell. Neighboring villages were already in German hands. She says she saw a German soldier just a few steps away from her. She said she wasn't afraid of him because they are people like we are. What did worry her most was that her party membership card might be found hidden in her stocking. She was certain that if she had been discovered, it would not have gone well for her. But everything turned out all right. She found her children. They rode part of the way back on a train, part in a truck, and in some places they traveled on foot. But she brought them through, alive and unharmed.

JULY 11

I received a call from Leningrad. Our house-management office proposes we leave with a transport for the Volga and Gorki. I declined the offer to go. All of these attempts at evacuation have not led to anything. I met Kholmyanskaya. She had been sent to Bologoye with a group of factory children after all. Airplanes flew over them the whole time and bombed them mercilessly. The terrified children screamed and cried, begging to go home to their parents. As a result, many mothers have now received leave to go after their children. Panic-stricken women fill the trains and stations, each one fighting to find her children and to whisk them to safety before the advancing enemy army.

I hear about the children at every turn. It seems to me that after such a terrible shock as war, concern for the children is the most worrisome, the keenest anxiety, an anxiety that can lead to insanity. My cousin Ludmilla has set off for the front line, near Staraya Russa. A month ago she sent her children there for the summer. Elizaveta Sergeyevna's husband who had gone after their three-year-old daughter appeared this morning. Good for him. As

14

a dependable worker,* he has the use of a car. This made it possible for him to circle through several villages and towns. Even so, he was lucky to find her. He brought her back, dressed only in a little undershirt. Not many in Leningrad have such luck as to find children sent away on summer vacation or evacuated ahead of the oncoming German danger by foresighted authorities.

JULY 14

In Tyarlevo I can sometimes forget about the war—how near it is—almost on top of us. But it is easy in the calm of nature, in these blissful summer days. I spent the day lying on the banks of Lake Pushkin. Blue sky, blue lake, and the green frame of the shoreline. It was peaceful. No voices were audible. No one strolling along the paths. Only somewhere, far away, the silvery walls of palaces sparkle through the greenery. It is even easy to forget everything that is happening in this tortured world. But not completely. From time to time, the sounds of warning signals penetrate the quiet and bring me back to reality.

JULY 18

Ration cards for bread, butter, and other products were introduced today. The quota for bread is 400 grams a day, for butter, 600 grams a month.† This is not so bad. One can live on this. Special commercial stores which are full of foodstuffs have been opened,

---

* *High party member* [ED.].
† *One Russian pound equals 409 grams; one American pound equals 454 grams* [ED.].

but the prices are very high. For instance, a kilogram of sugar costs seventeen rubles.* The prices of everything else are about just as high. People walk in, look at the prices and leave, empty-handed.

The problem is money. People have very little of it. Rarely did anyone put some aside for a rainy day. Even if someone does have substantial savings, he is not free to use them. On the very first day of the war came the edict that not more than 200 rubles per month could be withdrawn by each person from his savings account. With these inflated prices, not much can be bought with that.

I think that all of these stores have a psychological rather than a practical use. When you see a shop window full of products, you tend to disbelieve talk about an imminent famine. But thoughts about it do depress and frighten. We can remember the years before the "New Economic Policy," when the most delectable course of fare in Leningrad was horsemeat fried in castor oil, and the famine of '33 when entire villages died in the Ukraine.

I mentioned my fears to Irina Levitskaya. But she laughed at me. "Yes. Well, if something like that happens, you know you have hundreds of friends here in Leningrad. Your children will be quite safe. There is no reason to be pessimistic."

God willing.

* *One ruble equals about 10 cents. A very good secretary in Leningrad earned about 250 rubles a month in 1941* [ED.].

AUGUST 1

For almost two weeks now, I haven't opened this notebook. Apathy. I am in no mood to write about the same things over and over again. There is no ray of hope. How can there be when storm clouds are gathering? The news from the city is steadily more and more alarming. My husband's niece brought her small daughter for a visit. She managed to get some cookies through the ration line and so shared them with us. The children played peacefully, and for a moment it seemed as if the war and its horrors were far away. From her I found out about the rapid German onslaught. They are advancing rapidly on Leningrad.

We have decided to stay in the country until Luga is captured. And when it is, we will have to go back to the apartment in the city.

AUGUST 2

All you need is three hours in Leningrad, and you'll hear enough to completely upset what peace of mind you may have left, especially the talk about new evacuations. But this time they are letting mothers go with their children. However, the women have been so frightened by those first disastrously unsuccessful attempts that they use various illnesses to get a postponement. Our house administrator is a woman who takes a mother's grief to heart. She strongly urges me to leave Leningrad. My mother does not want to move, and I don't know what to do. There is still another fear—epidemics of typhoid, cholera, and other stomach disorders are raging along the roads. That, in addition to the fact that the evacuation trains are fired upon and exposed to bombardment. The family of the director of the factory where my husband worked, left. Soon after came the news that their fourteen-year-old son had died of typhoid fever. Kholmyanskaya had decided not to go anywhere. Her husband volunteered for service. Her older son, a twenty-year-old student, has been drafted. She is left alone with a small boy. She told me how, when her son was leaving, she begged him to kill himself rather than be taken prisoner since, according to rumors, the Germans kill every Jew they find.

I tried to visualize the grisly scene—a mother pleading with her son to commit suicide. Can it be possible that the Germans will kill someone just because he is a Jew? I cannot imagine it. But Kholmyanskaya is convinced. She begs me to hide her little boy in case of defeat and to say he is my relative. Certainly, I promised.

It appears that my husband will be kept in Leningrad. Mr. Kholmyanski wants him in his unit. But my husband has decided not to seek a transfer. He is a confirmed fatalist. He does not want to initiate anything. He firmly believes in his principle "What must be will be."

A few minutes before I was to leave Leningrad, Kholmyanski called me. Obviously with the best intentions, he decided to ask my support in his plans concerning my husband. He asked me if I knew of his proposal to my husband.

"Yes, I know."

"You must convince him, then. You must do this without delay."

"I understand and I thank you very much. But you know Sergey. He is an incurable fatalist."

"That's exactly why I am calling. Convince him. Do you understand, this is vital. In today's situation it is extremely important. And understand this, too—every day it will be worse and more difficult."

For ten minutes he stubbornly urged me to use my influence on my husband, pointing out the advantages tied to such a transfer to staff duty.

AUGUST 4

Only now, late at night, while writing this, do I come to the realization of what a long and hard day it has been. After a month and a half I am today, for the first time, really beginning to understand what war means. Right after I arrived in Leningrad, I learned that Kholmyanski is dead. I spent the whole morning running around with his wife to get an official confirmation of his death. Poor Faina is beside herself. Seeing her despair and remembering her husband with whom we had been such good friends, I, too, cannot hold back the tears. Finally we found all the details. Kholmyanski and his aide (the very position he had offered my husband), were driving in a car somewhere beyond the city limits. German airplanes began to shoot at them. They threw themselves out of the car and under the slope of a railroad embankment. A bomb fell right into the railbed and the two men were killed by falling rails, blown into the car.

I returned with Faina to their empty apartment. After some time, the doorbell rang. I opened the door for a student who had been a friend of the elder Kholmyanski boy. Pale and distraught, she called me to another room and told me that Dodick (the son) and his unit had been surrounded. We looked at each other dumbly, not knowing what to do, how to tell his mother. We decided to keep quiet for the time being. Maybe this is a mistake. Midnight. A waning moon has risen over the lake. It is deathly pale.

AUGUST 5

So far there have been no bombings. Marina's husband, Volodya, dropped in. He feels terribly important and proud of his rank as an officer of the active army. Armed to the teeth. He assures us authoritatively that no danger threatens Leningrad. The anti-aircraft defense system is so tremendous that not one airplane will be allowed through. Can that be?

Our acquaintances envy our relatively peaceful life in the country.

AUGUST 7

Spy-mania has hit the city. Every day they catch one here, find one there. As a rule, these spies turn out to law-abiding citizens who somehow accidently have aroused the suspicions of some very zealous "arm of the law." Even my poor Dima has been a victim. His height, his fair, curly hair, and particularly his glasses, must have provoked the suspicion of a militiaman. We were walking to the train station, and on the way I stopped at a store for a moment. Dima was waiting for me on the street. When I came out after a few minutes, I saw the militiaman demanding something from Dima, who was obviously petrified. I hurried to them. The militiaman was ready to take the boy to headquarters to clear up his identity since Dima did not have any documents with him. I had to argue with him and point out that Dima could not possibly have a passport because he is under sixteen.

To prove what I was saying, I dragged out all my papers and my husband's military certificate which, luckily, I had with me. I finally convinced him that Dima really is my son and not a German spy. He let him go. We will have to be more careful. It is dangerous for Dima to go out on the streets alone.

AUGUST 12

We left the cottage today, the last to go. All those who had risked a country vacation returned to the city previously. They say that Luga will be taken any day now. And from Luga to Leningrad it is just a stone's throw. I am worried about Dima. At fifteen, they could send him away to dig trenches.

And the Germans fly over and strafe. The trenches are senseless—a good way to kill people.

AUGUST 13

The evacuation continues; many are leaving. They are transferring entire factories along with their complete personnel. Now my decision to stay in the city haunts me. The stores haven't been full for a long time. People buy up everything, even the expensive items. Would it be better to leave?

AUGUST 15

As if in answer to my torturous question, a notice came today that I must evacuate Leningrad. I am allowed to take the whole family. I can even pick out the direction—either Gorki or the Caucasus. And again I hesitate.

If the war is really progressing at such a breakneck pace, then, probably, it will end soon. Why leave a settled place? Maybe it would be wiser to stay in the apartment? What to do?

AUGUST 17

At any rate, I went to the doctor and got a postponement until the 23rd of August. I have to gain some time to think over the situation. I can decide what to do peacefully with a few more days.

AUGUST 19

I spend all my free time running around getting food. It is very hard to get, even in the commercial stores. For instance, one can only buy a hundred grams of butter. But I want to lay up some sort of supplies somehow. That is why every day I must stand in several lines.

AUGUST 20

Detachments of evacuees leave for the East every day. Martinov, a former co-worker, came by to say good-bye. He is leaving for somewhere in the Urals with the Voroshilov factory. Theatres are leaving also. The Marinski has already been sent to Perm. All this only reinforces my alarm; doubts grow. I could be making an irreparable mistake, taking on myself the responsibility for the lives of my children and the whole family. But I must finally decide on something.

AUGUST 23

The last transport left during the night. Today, that route has been cut off. Leningrad is surrounded, and we have been caught in a mousetrap. What have I done with my indecision?

AUGUST 25

This fever to get food has reached an unbelievably high degree. Everything is virtually disappearing. By chance, you might accidentally overhear that in the Petrograd section of town they are distributing something or other. So you run there. After that, to Narvsky Gate. And then on to Vasilevski Island. You buy up everything you can lay your hands on. But there isn't really anything substantial or nourishing. The stores are all but empty. Everywhere there are enormous lines. And the crowds grow whenever sugar or butter appears in the commercial stores. Today I saw Irina's mother. She told me in a whisper that leaflets have been scattered everywhere. They say it is unnecessary to stock up for more than two weeks. After that the city will be surrendered. There are many who believe this.

AUGUST 28

In line from morning to night. Nothing new. We find ourselves in tense anticipation.

SEPTEMBER 1

All commercial stores were closed today. The ration quota has been lowered. Produce must be obtained by other means. Many drive out to fields not yet occupied by Germans and gather potatoes and vegetables left by the rural population.

SEPTEMBER 5

We have returned to prehistoric times: life has been reduced to one thing—the hunt for food. I took stock of our food supply. It will barely suffice for a month. It may be that later the situation will change. But for exactly what change I am hoping—I myself don't know. Now we are approaching the greatest horror—starvation. Tomorrow, Lubov Tarnovskaya and I are going to go outside the city to trade off the cigarettes and vodka we were able to buy at a kiosk.

SEPTEMBER 7

This morning Yura and I sat on a bench along the boulevard. Miloradovich, a former classmate of mine, sat down next to us. Without any introduction, he began talking about how happy he is that the Germans are just outside the city, that theirs is an inestimable power, and that if the city doesn't surrender today, then it will tomorrow. He praised me for not leaving. "And this is," he said, showing me a small revolver, "in case my hopes deceive me."

I did not know how to react to his words. We are accustomed to distrusting people. But there are many such as he, now. Impatiently they await the Germans as saviors.

24

When I returned home, I was greeted by my elderly uncle, a doctor from Pushkin. He had come to Leningrad several days before on the advice of friends, thinking it the safest and easiest place to survive the invasion of the Germans. But after looking things over, he decided to go back home. The trains are no longer running and the only means of travel left is walking. We tried to talk him out of it, but he remained firm. "Let me die in my own home." And a few minutes after he had gone, the air alarm sounded, and the antiaircraft artillery started its pounding.

This is the city's first air raid. It has made quite an impression. In the first place, our faith in Leningrad's being well protected has been shaken. Secondly, we can see for ourselves what a threat hangs over us. There are crowds around destroyed houses.

SEPTEMBER 8

I awoke with a gnawing feeling. Ominous foreboding. In the city they talk about the large number of leaflets scattered by the Germans. The content of these leaflets is an ultimatum. If the city has not surrendered by September 9, there will be a massive bombardment.

SEPTEMBER 9

Yesterday evening we were standing on the balcony, my mother, aunt, and I, discussing our hopeless situation. Suddenly our attention was attracted by several shiny dots in the sky which were rapidly coming straight at us. We didn't even have a chance to look them over when the alarm sounded. Time to run to the basement. Apparently they were reconnaissance planes since, soon after, the sirens sounded again, and after that there was heavy bombing. Houses crumbled. Yura slept soundly despite the noise. I hated to wake him. We do not have a very good shelter; the cellar is no safer than the apartment. But the din intensified. Whole new squadrons flew over us, bombs fell endlessly, and the antiaircraft artillery blasted at full power. Sheer hell. Our house could fall apart at any moment. I couldn't stand it—I grabbed my sleeping Yura and ran to the basement.

Down there are many people, especially children. They cry loudly, pressing closely to their panic-stricken mothers. With each new explosion, the women, many of whom are Communists, compulsively cross themselves and whisper prayers. In such moments, antireligious propaganda is forgotten.

It seemed that the bombardment would never end. Today we learned that our sector has suffered gravely; much is in ruins. Four large apartment buildings which all stood together in a row on our street have been destroyed. I looked at the neighboring stricken streets. A few scenes have etched themselves into my memory, probably until I die: a house demolished almost to its foundations, but one wall remained, still papered in the favorite cornflower design. There is even a picture hanging on it, as straight as ever. Above a heap of bricks, cement, and beams, a whole corner of an upper apartment of another house was preserved. In the corner, an icon; on the floor, toys, scattered everywhere as if the children had just finished playing. Further down was a room half buried under debris, but against the wall, a bed with fluffy pillows, and a lamp . . . household items, surviving by chance, open to the eyes of passersby—silent witnesses to the fact that someone or something alien tore mercilessly into the private life of people and barbarously defaced it.

SEPTEMBER 12

I am writing half an hour after the latest air raid. I don't know how long it all took, but a few minutes after the All Clear, we learned that just a few blocks from us a huge hospital had been hit. It was opened only yesterday, and today they transferred the wounded there. They say that the bombers dove just at that building. It burst into flames immediately. The majority of the wounded are dead. They couldn't get them out in time.

And all the time they told us that Leningrad was inaccessible, that there would be no air raids. This is how inaccessible it is! The antiaircraft defense might just as well be soap bubbles. Guarantee of safety? A shallow phrase.

SEPTEMBER 12, *evening*

Today we learned the grimmest consequence of today's bombing. The Badayevski warehouses are completely destroyed. All the supplies of the city were concentrated there. Isn't it strange that supplies were centered just in that spot, a spot well known to the entire city? The Germans, of course, were well informed of this. The destruction of this storehouse threatens Leningrad with inevitable starvation. The whole city is steeped in clouds of smoke and the odor of burning ham and charred sugar.

SEPTEMBER 15

The destruction of the Badayevski warehouses can already be felt. The daily ration of bread has been lowered to 250 grams. Since there is almost nothing else besides the bread, this decrease is felt strongly. I am still trying to get potatoes and vegetables from the surrounding villages by trading various items.

How tormenting it all is! I walked all day yesterday. I had cigarettes, my husband's boots, and ladies' shoes. I feel like a pitiful beggar. Everywhere I must beg, literally implore. The peasants are already overloaded with valuable things; they don't even want to talk. For a short time, the terrible year of 1918 returned. That year, the city people, like beggars, begged for potatoes and flour from the peasants in exchange for rugs, furs, jewelry, and other valuable items. Completely exhausted, I finally managed to exchange all my goods for sixteen kilos of potatoes and two liters of milk. I don't know how much longer I will be able to keep this up.

SEPTEMBER 20

It gets harder every day. This question of nourishment is the most important. Even daily air raids no longer make any special impression. We are used to them. Everyone is occupied with only one thought; where to get something edible so as not to starve to death.

The item most in demand for trade is alcohol. True, it is not of very good quality. But it is strong. Sometimes a nearby kiosk gets some of this repulsive, stinking liquid. There are long lines for this drink.

I, too, try not to miss any such lucky happening and patiently stand in the endless line. In one village, I found an old woman drunkard who is willing to give a fair number of potatoes for this trash. Lucky that there are still such old women around.

SEPTEMBER 25

Irina came by today, very upset, and gave us this sad news. Marina Tolbyzina, my friend from early childhood, is dead. Marina, a group of co-workers, and her inseparable maid, Tonya, were sent to dig trenches in the outskirts of Leningrad. Having worked its shift, the whole group was returning along the highway when a Red Army car caught up with them. Marina, utterly exhausted, begged a ride for herself and Tonya. The driver agreed. The car passed up the group and hadn't quite managed to make the bend in the road when, before everyone's eyes, it blew up. All this was accompanied by so much noise and smoke that it hid the machine from view. When the rest finally reached the scene, they could not find a trace of the passengers. It was impossible to stay to look for them since that part of the road became subject to heavy firing.

This is what we had to hear. We were saddened by the news of Marina—a young, lovely, and lively woman and her untimely death—and again we return to our everyday worries about saving our own lives.

SEPTEMBER 28

There are persistent rumors that the bread ration will be cut again. That would be catastrophic. In August, I managed to buy a few kilos of real coffee. Now this is our salvation. A few cups in the morning and I feel energetic the rest of the day.

A Tartar, who formerly bought old items, appeared today. He brought four bars of chocolate and sold them for money. This is a completely unbelievable event for these times, since money is not worth anything anymore. The only medium of exchange now, is goods. True, we paid 120 rubles for the chocolate—monthly wages for a janitor—but I consider the purchase a great success. This way I will be able to give the children at least a small piece every day.

OCTOBER 2

The new bread ration: 125 grams for white-collar workers and dependents, 250 for manual laborers. Our portion (125 grams) is a small slice, just enough for a sandwich. We have started dividing the bread equally among all. Everyone wants to use his own portion in his own way. For instance, my mother tries to stretch her piece into three meals. I eat my entire portion right away in the morning with the coffee so that I might have at least enough strength to stand in line or perhaps to make some sort of trade. In the afternoons though, I become weak and must lie down.

Today I dropped by to see a friend and learned that her husband died during the night. When I asked from what, she answered simply: "He starved to death." He had gone to bed in the evening and she naturally supposed that he had fallen asleep. But when she looked in the morning, he was dead. Does this await us all?

No changes at the front. The Germans have surrounded the city. They bomb daily with Germanic precision at exactly seven o'clock every evening. They probably want to starve us into submission. Immediately after the alarm signal, bombs literally pour down. Our defense system never warns us in time. Even though the basement is not really any protection at all, still the herd instinct and its security drives us below.

OCTOBER 6

The population in our apartment is growing. My cousin Ludmilla's children came and settled in the room already occupied by my aunt and uncle. The size of the room—a scant twelve square meters. How will they all be able to fit? There can't be enough air for everyone. Of course, no one is worried about that. Like animals, people cling to one another in time of danger. Ludmilla will also be coming in a few days. From the beginning of the war she has lived apart from her children. She is at work all day, and so the children stayed with a friend who doesn't work. But a few days ago, a bomb fell into that house. Fortunately, the children were in the basement. But even so, due to the bombing, the water pipes burst and the basement was flooded.

Today the Tartar again appeared. He brought a kilo of horsemeat in exchange for a bottle of red wine.

OCTOBER 8

People virtually turn into animals before our eyes. Who would have thought that Irina, always such a quiet, lovely woman, would be capable of beating her husband whom she always adored. And for what?

31

Because he wants to eat all the time and never can get enough. He just waits for her to bring something home, and then he throws himself on the food. Of course, she is hungry herself. But it is hard for a starving man to leave even one little piece.

The most grisly sight in our apartment is the Kurakin family. He, back from exile and emaciated by years in prison, is already beginning to bloat. It is simply horrible! There is little left of his wife's former love. She is constantly irritated and argumentative. Their children cry and beg for food. But all they get is spankings. However, the Kurakins are no exception. Almost everyone has changed as a result of hunger, the blockade, and this desperate situation.

My husband amazes me. He stands far above all those who have lost their sympathetic, humane outlooks. He is distinguished in that his attitude toward those around him has not changed. Soldiers' fare is also far from exceptional. For breakfast they receive a cup of watery porridge. But he doesn't eat it. He brings it home to Yura. He has one care—to help whom he can. Often he comes home during air raids, afraid that I won't go into the cellar. He is right. I don't especially believe in the protective quality of our cellar. To make him happy, I usually take the boys and crowd down into the basement with the rest of the household. Lately we have had to stay there from seven in the evening to twelve at night. The Germans do not give us any respite and drag out the bombardment through several hours. At least when you finally do go to bed, you don't feel quite so hungry. That is why I try to avoid these trips to the basement and go to bed early. Often, in dreams, you picture a table full of all sorts of snacks, lots of delicious things. You don't want to wake up. And when you do, it's gloomy reality and the gnawing feeling of hunger again.

Will we survive? My only wish is not to lose the children. I don't want to see them die.

OCTOBER 12

The potatoes ran out today. Our grain supply gave out earlier. It is impossible to get anything in the co-operatives by ration card. And the lines are colossal whenever anything edible does appear on sale, even if it's not very nourishing. The strong defeat the weak. Women almost never get into the stores. Sometimes the lines start at four in the morning. My husband suggested getting me a pass into the military mess hall where one can get lunches instead of the supplies normally available by ration cards. For our family this is eight plates of soup and four plates of porridge for ten days. Of course, this is better than nothing.

OCTOBER 18

For a few days now, I have had an extra job—that of bringing the dinner from the mess hall. I take two cans and set off for a long journey which terminates in standing in line for several hours. At home we dilute the soup with water. It is hard to make the coupons last ten days. Going to the country is out of the question. Those trips have lost their usefulness. The peasants have stopped trading. They, too, are afraid that they will be left with nothing.

OCTOBER 26

Today is Dima's birthday. Ludmilla, who works in the mess hall, brought him some wild fowl as a present. What a feast that was!

OCTOBER 28

Irina Levitskaya's husband died. She didn't even grieve.

NOVEMBER 1

Every day it's the same thing. The sirens scream at around seven every night. My mother hurries to eat supper at six and then gathers up all the essential things and sits, prepared, in her coat. She assures me that this reminds her of getting ready for Easter matins. When the alarm sounds, we trudge downstairs. Our neighbors move our ailing uncle, chair and all. Old women descend, groaning. Our former landlady who so impatiently awaits the Germans, complains the most. Then the bombs. And the loveliest, finest city in the entire country is being destroyed.

NOVEMBER 3

My typewriter broke down, and I can't get it fixed. No one is left to do it. Men are generally disabled; many of them have already taken to their beds, weak from hunger. Our janitor has not been able to get up for a long time now. In general, no yard is in order. Disgusting neglect everywhere.

Nearly every day there is news of the death of one acquaintance or another. Several people have died in our building too.

We are hoping that there will be some sort of food distribution in celebration of November 7.* There is a lot of talk about it. They are hoping for butter, wine, and sweets.

NOVEMBER 6

Tarnovskaya got up this morning at four. With the help of her son and energetic daughter-in-law, she forced herself into a cooperative, and got herself and us some butter. Absolutely unbelievable! We are torn by the wish to eat it all at once and the realization that we must stretch it out somehow.

Since the 20th of October Dima has been "working" fictitiously in a workshop, thanks to George Tarnovski. Although that workshop is still being organized, Dima is already considered a worker and receives 250 grams of bread a day instead of the 125 gram ration. This is very important for Dima. He always did have a big appetite, and when the rationing started, he weakened quickly. His apathy has me in despair. He has lost interest in everything. He won't read or talk. It is hard to believe but he is even indifferent to the bombings. The only thing that can bring him out of it is food. He is hungry all day and rattles around through the cupboard, looking for food. When he can't find anything, he chews on coffee grounds or those abominable oil cakes which were once fed only to the cattle.

---

* *November 7 is the anniversary of the Bolshevik Revolution* [ED.].

All of Leningrad eats oil cake now. They pay whatever is asked for it: shoes, stockings, pieces of material. You take any valuable article to the market-place, and you get this substance in exchange. It is so coarse that you can't bite into it. You can't even cut it up with an axe. You have to shave it like a piece of wood to get something like sawdust. And from this you bake pancakes. They are extremely unappetiz-ing. And after you eat them—heartburn. The bread, too, is barely edible. There is a minimal percent of flour in it. Mostly it consists of oil cake, celluloid, and some other unknown substance. As a result of these ingredients the bread is dry and heavy. Nevertheless, people are ready to cut each other's throats for it. In the morning, on the way home from the bakery, you must hide it carefully. There have been many in-stances in which the bread has been stolen right on the street.

NOVEMBER 7

As we expected, the Germans bombed more inten-sively and mercilessly than usual during the Novem-ber holidays. They were especially severe last night. Clouds of planes flew over us. The air hummed from the multitude of planes.

For the hundredth and thousandth time I asked myself the question: Where is our antiaircraft de-fense system? Where are the Soviet gunners? The Germans fly around as if they were at home; our ar-tillery blasts at them in vain and only intensifies the noise.

Today Tarnovskaya and I tried to bring life back to Dima. Zoya is energetic and has not lost her opti-mism. She firmly believes that the war will end soon and that Leningrad ultimately will be captured by the

Germans after all. We will have to endure just a little while longer. She tried to impress this all on Dima; she even yelled and screamed at him. Then she pleaded with him that he perk up for my sake, that he be more cheerful toward everyone. I supported her as much as I could, but nevertheless, we could make no headway.

Now people die so simply. At first the person loses all interest in everything; he goes to bed and never gets up again. That is why I fear this apathy in Dima. I can't recognize him. Even at the end of August and in September he walked around the city searching for products, interested himself with military communiques, and met with his friends. Now he seems like an old man, constantly freezing. He spends whole days standing by the stove in a winter jacket, pale, with deep, blue circles under his eyes. If this continues, he will die. I do everything possible to feed him better, but there is just not enough. George Tarnovski, who is now living in our apartment, for instance, goes to the mess hall every day to eat from six to seven bowls of yeast soup which is obtainable without ration cards. This "special delicacy" of starving Leningrad is hard to imagine—yeast and water. After eating it, people swell. It is not in the least bit nourishing. It has absolutely no calories. But I wish Dima would show some interest in getting this soup. Maybe this would bring him out of his terrible indifference.

NOVEMBER 10

We are virtually being buried under incendiary bombs. Earlier, all the little boys in our apartment house would stand guard on the roof—Dima's friend Sergei, Dima, the son of the actress on the third floor

—a bright and healthy boy—and many others—all between 12 and 16 years of age. Now nearly all of them are ill. Someone must fight the effects of the bombs, and women have proved to be the most durable. Yesterday our woodshed caught fire, but we were able to put it out. The only casualty of that fire turned out to be the mattress we had carried out there for lack of space in the house. It's a good thing that the firewood brought to us just yesterday didn't burn.

NOVEMBER 12

I dropped in on an acquaintance and she treated me to the latest culinary creation: jelly made of leather straps. The recipe is as follows: boil pig's hide straps and then prepare something on the order of jellied meat. This mess is beyond description—yellow and repugnant. As hungry as I was, I couldn't swallow even one spoonful. I choked. My friends are surprised at my disgust. They eat it all the time. They say that it is sold in great quantities at the marketplace. However, I don't go there anymore. I have nothing left to trade. Anything I might have to offer wouldn't interest anyone.

The markets are overloaded with beautiful things: quality materials, materials for suits and coats, costly dresses, furs. These are the only items that will buy bread and vegetable oil.

Not just rumors, but reliable sources, i.e., news from militia sectors, tell us that a lot of sausage has appeared at the marketplace—jellied meat and such —made of human flesh. To think that such a horrible possibility could be imagined! People have reached their limits and are capable of everything. My husband has already warned me not to let Yura wander far from home even with nana for children are the first to disappear.

NOVEMBER 15

Death reigns in the city. People die and die. Today, as I made my way along the street, a man was walking ahead of me. He could barely put one foot in front of the other. Passing him, I reluctantly turned my attention to his blue, cadaverous face. I thought to myself that he would surely die soon. Here, certainly, one could say that death had placed its stamp on the face of this man. After several steps, I turned around and stopped to watch him. He sat down on a hydrant, his eyes rolled back, and then he slowly slipped to the ground. When I finally reached him, he was already dead.

People are so weak from hunger that they are completely indifferent to death. They die as if they are falling asleep. Those half-dead people who are still around do not even pay any attention to them. Death has become a phenomenon observable at every turn. People are used to it. They are apathetic, knowing that such a fate awaits everyone, if not today, then tomorrow. When you leave the house in the morning, you come upon corpses lying in the streets. The corpses lie around for a long time since there is no one to take them away.

NOVEMBER 20

My husband has arranged with the head of the hospital on the Petrograd side. They will use Dima as a courier. Dima will be given a breakfast of soup. This is very important. It is likely that this job will save

Dima and it will distract him. The main thing is that he will receive additional food. I no longer have the means to give him anything beyond the morning meal. Our menu has dwindled to morning coffee with a portion of bread distributed every day. Later, at six, we have the soup I bring from the canteen.

The doctors maintain that if we take a bath twice a week and drink three glasses of some liquid every day, we can survive several months. I doubt this very much. This prescription may work if you rest all the time, but I have to be on the go constantly to obtain even that minimal bit necessary to maintain life. You stand in line for hours for one loaf of bread. Sometimes you may have to go to several bakeries since there are shortages. The water mains are cracking, and it is necessary to go to the Neva for water. All this demands of the citizens of Leningrad an over-extension of what little strength they do have. What trouble just the firewood causes! There is no one to help with it when it is finally delivered and left in the yard. All the cutting, sawing, and carrying it to sheds and to apartments have become the responsibilities of women. Two people carry out these tasks at our house —nana, who still manages to walk, and little Yura, who has weakened less than anyone else. So the two of them saw, cut up, and drag the heavy, raw, frozen logs. Yura and nana even take care of the courtyard since our janitor has been ill for a long time now, and apparently hopelessly so. In such a way Yura, who is not yet six years old, works like an adult.

NOVEMBER 24

Dima absolutely refuses to go to the basement during air raids. He returns from work so tired that he can't move. Right after eating, he goes to bed and begs not to be disturbed. Something in his job is not working out the way it was supposed to. His duties as courier take him quite far. The hospital sends him to various ends of the city, and often the streetcars are not running. To top it off they even omit his supper. The head of the kitchen even tries to save on that bowl of soup agreed upon. Only when Dima shows up with the director's son, does he get everything—even cutlets. No wonder *that* boy is so well nourished and rosy cheeked. He doesn't look like a Leningrad citizen.

NOVEMBER 26

Unexpectedly, a completely strange Red Army soldier knocked on our door and gave us a pail of sauerkraut which he carried with great caution. This is certainly an event, but we will have to eat it without bread or potatoes for we have neither.

The death rate grows. They say that as many as 3,000 people die daily. I don't think this is an exaggeration. The city is literally flooded with corpses. Relatives or friends take them to be buried, tied on by twos and threes to small sleds. Sometimes you come across larger sleighs on which the corpses are piled high like firewood and covered over by a canvas. Bare, blue legs protrude from beneath the canvas. You can be certain this is *not* firewood.

You observe death so closely every day that you stop reacting to it. The feeling of pity has vanished. No one cares. The worst thing is the harsh realization that it is scarcely likely that we will escape the common fate. Sooner or later they will carry us out and throw us into a common grave. It is impossible to bury each corpse separately. There aren't enough coffins. If relatives want to have a proper funeral, they must wait until a coffin is freed, that is, until the preceding corpse is driven to the gravesite, taken out of his coffin, buried, and the coffin handed down to those next in line.

NOVEMBER 29

My former maid, Marusa, appeared unexpectedly, unexplainedly. She brought a loaf of bread and a voluminous sack of cereal. Marusa is unrecognizable. She is not the same barefoot, unkempt girl I knew. She wore a squirrel jacket, an attractive silk dress, and an expensive scarf. Added to all this, a blooming appearance . . . just as if she had come from a vacation. She is not at all a citizen of a hungry, embattled city. I asked why. It turns out that the reason is very simple. She works in a food warehouse. The director of the warehouse is in love with her. Whenever the workers are searched before they leave, Marusa is searched just for the sake of appearance. She carries out several kilos of butter, sacks of cereal, rice, and canned goods—all hidden under her fur jacket. Sometimes, she says, she has even managed to take out several chickens. She takes everything home, and in the evenings the director comes to eat and relax. At first Marusa lived in a dormitory. Then her brigade leader made her aware of the advantages of joint living and invited Marusa to live with her. Now this woman makes use of Marusa's rich harvest to feed her own relatives and friends. Obviously, she is a very clever person. She has completely taken charge of foolish and good-hearted Marusa and under the guise of a kindly person exchanges Marusa's food products for various things. Thus, Marusa's wardrobe has improved. She is delighted over these trades and little interests herself with where her precious booty goes. Marusa told me all this naïvely, adding that now she will try to see to it that my children did not go hungry.

Writing this, I have to think about what is happening in our unfortunate, besieged city. Thousands of people die daily, but some people have the richest comforts even under these conditions. True, during Marusa's visit I did not consider these things. Moreover, I begged her not to forget us and offered her anything which might interest her.

DECEMBER 1

Our beloved janitor is very ill. Today I took him some porridge made of the cereal Marusa brought. He can't praise Yura enough. He says, "I can be sick in peace. Yura will work for me."

DECEMBER 6

Last night we lived through something we had not endured up to now. I went to bed at around ten and turned off the radio as I usually do so I wouldn't hear the broadcast alarm. Recently, I have felt my strength fail me. I am not in any condition to spend the evening and part of the night on a chair in the basement, swaying from sleepiness. Because of this there have been a few unpleasant "discussions" with my cousin Ludmilla who lives with us and sleeps in the room next to mine. She is afraid she will sleep through the alarms. At the first signal, she rushes to the basement, dragging her children with her. Yesterday she didn't notice my maneuver and went to bed. At eleven, I was awakened by intense crashing and

banging. I decided that the house would be destroyed
and that we would perish under the ruins. The force
of the blast tore down the curtains. Pictures fell from
the walls. From the street came cries for help. I
jumped out of bed, grabbed sleeping Yura, ready to
run any which way, not really knowing just where I
could run. I found myself in the hall. There was complete confusion. People were running, shouting, crying. Everything was in a muddle. After a few minutes we learned that a huge bomb had fallen into the
neighboring building. Windows were knocked out all
over the block. Window frames and doors were torn
out. Many were killed or hurt. All the able-bodied
people in our house ran to give aid to the victims. A
first-aid station was set up in our basement. Groaning, injured people were carried in. Children were
gathered from along the entire block. They were
screaming and crying. And the air raid sirens continued to wail. Bombs fell endlessly. It was not until
two A.M. that we returned to our apartment. It is unrecognizable. All the windows are broken out and the
floor is covered with glass splinters. It is as cold inside as out. There is nowhere to sleep. We barely
settled ourselves in the kitchen and in the hall. I
didn't close my eyes once before morning.

DECEMBER 7

To all these discomforts has been added one more—
complete darkness. There can not even be any talk
of putting in new glass; Leningrad windows have
long been boarded up with plywood. The cold is
cruel. There is no more firewood. How will we be
able to heat our apartment? The only thing we had
left to us were cozy rooms. Now we have even been

deprived of that. What more will we have to endure?

It is so painful to look at the elderly living in our apartment. Our former landlady, Anastasia Vladimirovna, who so sarcastically smiled on the first night of the war, is now slowly dying. Yet she is full of hope that she will survive these terrible days. More than anything, she is afraid that we will be able to evacuate, one way or another, and she will be left alone. While we are here she still gets her bowl of soup and I bring her that microscopic piece of bread for which I stand in line. In such a way she survives. If we leave, it will be her end. Despite this hopeless situation, she nevertheless does not want to die. She is eager for the end of the war and a German victory.

There is still another aged woman, an Estonian, Karolina. Once she was employed as a housekeeper by a Russian prince. Now she receives a lifetime pension from the former manager of the prince's family. The pension allows her to live reasonably well in her remaining postrevolutionary years. Besides this pension, she also receives a Soviet one—fourteen rubles per month. These rubles are enough to pay her rent and electricity bill. But thanks to foreign assistance, she has enough money. For instance, knowing that one can get bread through the "black market" (600 rubles per kilo), she asked me to get some for her.

After I carried out her request, a small tragedy occurred. The bread was sliced and placed on the stove to make toast when the neighbor's daughter stole several slices. The old woman's grief is hard to describe. All day she lies on the kitchen table—the windows are out in her room, too—and groans endlessly, talking constantly of the lost bread. Probably if someone very dear to her had died, she would not grieve nearly so much.

DECEMBER 10

Our kitchen is the scene of something unbelievable. Four housewives try to prepare their meals on one stove. They boil the oil cakes, baking pancakes from them, heat soup brought from the mess hall, argue, groan, and complain of the lack of food. The children are right there to hear it all, and it isn't possible to shoo them out of the warm kitchen. One who is especially annoying is Kurakin's oldest daughter, who had had light fingers before and now even more so — always looking to steal something from the neighbors. The women are afraid to move a step from their meager preparations. The electricity is out. The kitchen is half dark. It is hard to keep track of "pillagers" like young Kurakina.

DECEMBER 15

Dima has taken sick leave. He no longer has the strength to go to work. Yesterday my husband accidentally met him on the street. The boy was falling into a snowbank, raising himself with difficulty and falling again. It's a good thing that he bumped into his father, who managed to take him and drag him home. Otherwise, alone, he would never have gotten home. He would have died like thousands die every day on the streets of Leningrad. I, myself, more than anything am afraid of sitting down to rest on the street, although I literally drop from exhaustion.

I convinced Dima to go to the hospital. He returned in terrible condition. The hospital is full of corpses. They lie on the floors, on the stairways, in all the passageways. Dima could not even step over them and he hurried back home.

DECEMBER 16

Dima has gone to his bed once and for all. He lies quietly and won't talk at all, burying his face in the pillow. Now he no longer gets up to search for food in the cupboards and buffet. It could be that he is convinced there is nothing in the house. Or it could be that he no longer has the strength. I look at him in horror. I am afraid that he will die. How can he survive this hunger? He is so tall and thin and unbelievably pitiful. I can't recognize the boy. Not long ago he was bubbling with life. He ran to school, was an excellent student, and was interested in everything.

DECEMBER 17

The alarms and air raids have stopped. They say it is because of the cold. However the mood does not improve. Starvation and death grow with each new day. Last night Ludmilla returned home quite upset. It was already dark when she started home from work. She was in a hurry. Suddenly a woman threw herself at Ludmilla and hung on her hand. At first Ludmilla was totally bewildered, but the woman explained thickly that she was extremely weak and could go no further. She asked for help. Ludmilla said that she herself had barely enough strength to get home. But the woman persisted, hanging on like a leech. Ludmilla tried desperately to free herself but somehow couldn't. The woman, grasping Ludmilla's hand, dragged her in the direction opposite our apartment. Finally, Ludmilla tore herself away, tripping over snowbanks. She started to run. When I opened the door for her, she was a ghastly sight—pale, her eyes full of terror, barely able to catch her breath.

Telling about what happened, she repeated over and over, "She will die. I know it. She will die today." I could guess the two conflicting emotions which fought within her: joy that she had escaped, that she was alive, and the horrifying thoughts about the woman she had had to leave to fate and to a certain death on this freezing December night.

DECEMBER 26

Our neighbor Karolina died. Her savings from the "royal" pension could not save her. Before her death, we pooled our strength and carried her from the kitchen where she lay on the table, into a room where the windows are boarded up with plywood. Wrapped in kerchiefs, shawls, and blankets, the old woman survived several days. She continually mumbled Estonian prayers. Or perhaps they were curses. It is so bizarre to enter her room, walk up to her and check to see if she is still alive. I fought hard to keep control of myself when I looked at this creature, already losing her human appearance.

Last night I was able to use my ration cards to get some sardines. Since I also had Karolina's card, I decided to try to feed her. It is hard to imagine how greedily she, a near-corpse, gulped the food. It was pathetic to look at how she stuffed her mouth with those sardines. She died an hour later.

DECEMBER 28

Dead Karolina has lain in her bed for two days now. There is no one to bury her. We tried to get her relatives, but they do not come. The militia and building management can't take care of all the corpses. What more will happen to our city if the death rate continues to grow?

People stand in lines gloomily and in silence. There are not even the usual arguments. Everyone is dull, weak, and exhausted to the point of complete indifference to anything that might happen to them.

DECEMBER 29

Today at dawn I was awakened by my neighbor Kurakina's cry, "Hurry. Wake up. Bread. There's a supplement!"

There had been much talk about this long-awaited increase. But no one believed it. So it turns out that we did get one. Dependents will get 200 grams; workers will get 350. But this won't save many people now.

JANUARY 1, 1942

Yesterday we celebrated New Year's Eve. It was hard to imagine a more grim "celebration." We have nothing left from the holiday distribution which was a meager one at that. They gave each family a bottle of red wine and a small bag of candy. We decided not to wait for the traditional twelve o'clock. We went to bed at ten. We sleep in a room whose windows are boarded with plywood. We don't undress to go to bed, but quite the opposite. We pull on everything we can. I, for instance, sleep in a fur jacket, a large kerchief and boots, and on top I cover myself with blankets. Yura's little bed is next to mine. Only his nose peeks out from beneath the covers. I listen to his breathing to be sure he is still alive.

Around twelve, a noise woke me. I saw my husband. He was sitting at the table in his military coat in front of one little burning candle, hunched, tired, staring into space. The heart bursts with pity for him, for us, for all the others caught in this mouse-trap. In front of my husband on the table lay three pieces of black bread. He brought these as a New Year's treat. He wanted to spend this evening with his family. There is a saying—"Those with whom you celebrate New Year's Eve, you will stay with the whole year." This night I didn't sleep. Thoughts turned in my head and wouldn't give me any peace. It seems demeaning and absurd to die of hunger, and there is no hope for a safe escape. Our strength fades with every day.

JANUARY 3

On the way to the mess hall I dropped in on my very good friend and also dressmaker, Nadezhda Ivanovna. Several days ago she visited us and, seeing Dima's condition, tried to cheer him up, promising great changes. "Pull yourself together, Dima. Soon it will be better. They'll give us more bread. Didn't you hear that there is fighting just beyond Tikhvin? Then there will be a road out of Leningrad."

Dima remained dully silent. He won't believe any-thing anymore. But Nadezhda Ivanovna's cheery tone and confidence worked on me. I decided to visit her today to raise my spirits a little. It is important to hear a reassuring word. When I rang the bell, her older sister answered. She led me silently to the din-ing room and she seemed to me to be almost un-balanced. On the table stood two coffins. In one lay my dear and lighthearted friend, Nadezhda Ivanovna, and in the other, her younger sister whom I also had seen in apparent good health only a few days ago.

JANUARY 6

Today I visited our good friends, the Levitskis. The moment I saw Irina's father, my heart was pressed by a bad presentiment. He looks like a candidate for the next world. He can't last long. He is dying gradually; this is how everyone has died—those with whom we spent our youth, with whom we had shared many years of happy memories. And now I look at Nikolai Georgevich, who no longer has the strength to move, who is incapable of doing anything. His wife is fuming. She wants him to go somewhere and cut firewood. The scene was so depressing that I hurried away.

I learned that a few days ago, Nikolai's sister died. No one had told us. But then, there wasn't any sense in it. No one goes to the cemetery anymore. No one has the energy and besides that, there is a sharp frost.

JANUARY 7

Approximately an hour ago, my husband's friend, Peter Yakovlevich Ivanov, dropped by. He was always a gay, lively young man, but now he is unrecognizable and surprised me by his thin, pale appearance and by his strange questions. Hunger changes everyone. He came to find out if the large gray cat which belonged to an actress living in our apartment house was still alive. He was in hopes that the cat had not yet been eaten since he knew how much the actress adored it. I had to disappoint him. There is not one living creature besides people who can barely walk left in our house. All animals have been eaten either by occupants of our house or by our agile neighbors.

And the actress's son started the whole business in the first place. He particularly took part in hunting birds, caught what he could and then went over to dogs and cats. I am certain that he did not spare his mother's pet, especially since it was a very large and fat cat.

In Leningrad, now, you will not see either cats or dogs. I must say, so far we haven't partaken of this "delicacy"—not because we haven't wanted to, but because we never caught one.

Yesterday on the street I bumped into my good friend, Fedor Mikhailovich, the father of that unfortunate little tubercular boy whom Irina and I were going to visit in Pushkin on the first day of the war. I was amazed at his appearance. He walks with a cane, looks like a very old man, and he is not yet forty years old. He told me that on Irina's request he searched out a cat and took it to her. It is hard to imagine that Irina, who not so long ago made fun of everyone's fears of starvation and assured us that in Leningrad there would always be people who would help, has now been reduced to eating cats.

Of course, Irina never thought that everyone would be subject to starvation. The exceptions are only certain important officials and those few who work in various warehouses and distribution centers.

Fedor has managed to survive because the Tartar sells him bread at 600 rubles a pound.* Black market prices are rising.

JANUARY 8

It has been almost two weeks since Karolina's death, and she is still lying on her bed. There is no one to

---

* *Russian pounds* [ED.].

bury her. Thanks to the harsh cold and broken out windows, her corpse has not decomposed. But how long can this go on?

Dima has finally been placed in the hospital. My husband did everything possible and with great difficulty got Dima a place in an infirmary for wounded soldiers. Since there are no more sources of transportation, I had to take the boy to the Petrograd side on foot. The trip was a horrible nightmare. Dima could barely move his swollen feet and leaned heavily on me. He looks so bad that even our citizens who are used to all sights, stared at us. Dima's face is blueblack and swollen; his eyes are dull. We walked for three whole hours. Of course at the hospital there were all sorts of complications. There was no vacant cot, so Dima was placed in the hall. Besides this, I had to fill out a great many forms. I am very afraid that Dima won't get better. I stopped by the room of the head of the hospital—Eshkelev. His son lives with him, a healthy, rosy-cheeked boy, who, despite the late hour, was still in bed and munched ham and cheese sandwiches. I couldn't believe my eyes, but it was so. We had already forgotten what ham and cheese looked like. Seeing my incredulity, his father put together a story that the boy had nearly died after losing his ration card. Afraid to confess it, he supposedly had not eaten anything for nearly two weeks. I thought about all the unfortunate wounded and sick who were lying in the hospital halls, about the people from whom this official, by utilizing his position, was taking food to feed his own healthy son.

But this is going on all around us. Everyone who has power or is in a position to deal with foodstuffs, uses his privileged place to the utmost. It makes no difference to them that people die like flies. And I am a good one, too—expressing my sympathies for the son because Dima's life depends on this "father-official."

JANUARY 13

Karolina has finally been buried. Our energetic house manager found the dead woman's niece and worked on her to act accordingly. Shortly, the niece appeared with a coffin and took her away. The occupants of our apartment are overjoyed—the corpse is gone.

Today, walking back from the mess hall, I was struck to see that literally at every step there are children's sleds carrying corpses. Corpses line the streets, their bare feet protruding from the snow drifts. Corpses do not need shoes. To think that there are people who somehow get advantages and benefit even in these terrible times. Since the beginning of the bombings there have appeared "specialists," whose only occupation is looting damaged homes and corpses. They are fully satiated and flourishing. Incidentally, there are such elements even in our house. Once they were a poor family. But since the very beginning of the war, the head of this family went to work at digging. And now they are unrecognizable, dressed in silk and fur and full every day.

JANUARY 15

Friends found me a position in a sewing workshop. This puts me in the first category as far as rationing goes. True, the workshop does very little; there is no light or fuel, but they give out the rations just the same. In this way I get a little bit more bread, and now every little crumb is vital.

JANUARY 16

Today I went to the dispensary. I was horrified at what I saw. The clinic is full of workers and laborers who are so weak that they can no longer work. But they are afraid of being accused of shirking, so they come after sickness excuses. At the clinic, many die waiting in line to see a doctor. In the full sense of the word, the floor in this establishment is piled with dead or dying. They can't take them away fast enough.

JANUARY 18

I never thought that visiting Dima in the hospital would demand so much strength. It is simply a chore. After spending several hours in line and bringing the family supper, I must immediately set off for the hospital. Sometimes it seems as if my strength deserts me completely. And Dima does not cheer me up, either. He is not improving. Pale and swollen, he still lies in the corridor; he shows absolutely no interest in life. Today he apathetically told me that yesterday, two young soldiers, ill with dystrophy, were brought to the hospital. In several hours these boys were dead. This means the army is racked by starvation, too.

Dima is covered with boils. One boil was lanced, but the wound will not heal. The body has weakened beyond belief. The hospital performs almost no operations—blood will not clot. At least where Dima is, there has not yet been an epidemic of dysentery. In other infirmaries, nearly all of the patients suffer from this disease.

JANUARY 19

Knowledgeable people say that the air raids have stopped because of the terrible cold. The fuel in the airplanes freezes. Besides this, our guards, despite their own complete exhaustion, continue at their posts. This is distinctly reminiscent of the recent past when almost everyone was mobilized to "fight" the incendiary bombs. People stood on rooftops and had to throw the bombs into tubs of sand. And the sand boiled from the thousand-degree heat. Now there are no incendiary bombs, but guards sit and wait for a signal anyway. Gray-haired oldsters, thin as laths, pull on as much clothing as possible and, wrapped in shawls tied behind their backs, they sit everywhere; by gates, in doorways, in halls, on stairways in anticipation of sudden alarm.

I remembered how Yura played war at Tyarlevo. He had gotten a Red Army cap somewhere, and he paraded around in it even though it went down over his ears. War always places the military in the forefront—this is a law. However, during this half-year, the Soviet army has not lived up to the faith placed in it.

JANUARY 20

I went to see Dima. He was just having supper. It turns out that in this hospital he does get something: watery millet soup and fifteen grams of fat in the morning; 300 grams of bread for the whole day; at twelve, soup again and occasionally a watery porridge with some sort of sauce; and another bowl of liquid in the evening. At least he eats three times a day. Surely, it isn't very nourishing. It won't make him well. Dima's appearance is not improving. Apathy. I am afraid that he may die.

Returning from the hospital, I wandered through the part on the Petrograd side. For a few minutes I tore myself away from reality. I thought about the past. Of course the hardships of life in the Soviet Union were excessive. The constant struggle for daily bread. And worst of all—oppression and fear. Constant fear for one's self and one's family. But there were pleasant, happy times, too, and I think the primary reason for them was the atmosphere my native and beloved city creates. I can remember how often it delighted me. Especially how the St. Isaac cupola, the spire of Peter-Paul fortress and the blue cupola of the mosque glowed beneath the setting sun in late April and early May. I loved my city in the winter—the snowy cover on the Neva ice, gardens and parks sparkling with frost, the crisp air fragrant with winter apples. Tonight is also a marvelous winter evening. The same Neva. The same parks. But my heart is wrung by agonizing grief, by the hopelessness of our situation, by not being able to believe in anyone or anything.

Sadly I made my way home. Dark, cold, a dying candle lighting our kitchen. And around this weak flame, all the occupants of our apartment—hungry, cross, on the verge of quarrel. There is little humanity left in people.

JANUARY 24

A new problem—fires. Every day something burns down. Today, on the way to see Dima, I saw a crowd standing around a house which blazed quickly and fiercely before my eyes. Many stood around, but no one tried to put it out. It seemed as though the spectacle amused them. When I returned in three hours, a pile of smoldering beams stood in place of the house. It couldn't have been otherwise. How and with what could it have been put out? There is no water. The fire brigades are not in any condition to deal with these fires. Huge houses burn down to the foundations. They say the fires occur because of the makeshift stoves whose pipes go right out through the windows. Of course the setup is primitive. Unwisely, everything that is near the stove is flammable.

We are shelled regularly by distant German artillery. The shellings destroy houses and whole blocks. You walk along the street and you can hear the steadily growing whistle. It has become a habit. You cling to the side of the street from which the shelling comes. Last night I had to go along the Fontanka, when they began shooting along the river. It was just as dangerous on one side of the street as on the other. Shells were flying over my head, exploding here and there. I thought I was used to everything, but it was difficult not to panic in this instance.

I never thought I could be so indifferent to death. I loved life, delighted myself with even its smallest pleasure. Everyone considered me a great optimist. But today I can only doubt that we will survive. I can muster no horror over the possibility of death.

Again there are rumors of evacuation. Many set off on foot across frozen Lake Ladoga. Mostly adolescents try it. Many die on the lake. The emaciated, weakened organisms cannot withstand the terrible cold.

JANUARY 25

Bread shortages in rationing are more frequent now. Lines form at four in the morning, and at nine there is still no bread. Today I stood for twelve hours—six to six—and only then did I get our ration. Varya, my aunt's maid, stood in line with me. When we came out of the bakery, she asked my permission to lean on my arm. She couldn't manage alone. I took her home. She lay down in the kitchen in a large utility basket where it is warmer.

JANUARY 26

Varya is dead. It happened in the kitchen in the same basket she had squeezed into last night. How and when, no one knows. We walked into the kitchen in the morning and were surprised that she was sleeping so late. Then we tried to wake her up, we discovered she was already cold. The children walk by the basket, bumping into the corpse. We hurried to drag Varya into Karolina's room, to that bed where her corpse had lain for two weeks. We all had to take a hand in moving her since none of us is very strong anymore. My mother walked ahead with a candle-end, lighting the corridor. The rest carried the dead woman: someone took the shoulders, someone the head, and someone else the feet. Now there is so much death in the house that our house-manager is practically helpless. But the big concern is the ration card. In the past it was necessary to turn it in just as soon as that person died. People would try to cover up the death for at least a few days so that they could use the additional card. Now there is a special policy. Relatives of the deceased may keep his card for ten days and use it to pay for the funeral. No one will dig a grave for money. Generally, relatives pay for the digging of a common grave with bread, which is cheaper, and in such a way they can feed their families at the corpses's expense. People resort to various tricks to prolong their own lives.

JANUARY 27

Today there is no bread—none of the bakeries baked their quotas. And on such a black day, something lucky just had to happen. As if it were willed, Marusa showed up. For a piece of dress material, a chiffon blouse and some other small things, she brought me four kilograms of rice. We cooked a huge pot of rice porridge. Marusa wants a gold wristwatch. Unfortunately, I do not have one to give her, either. Marusa gave me her ration card. But I can't get any use out of this present. The coops are empty and the mess hall does not go by ration cards. It only takes care of soldier's dependents. Attempting to use the card can only get me into a lot of trouble.

Getting dinner from the mess hall takes up half the day. These are the bleakest days of my life.

JANUARY 29

Rumors about a possible evacuation are becoming more and more persistent. My uncle, who is so weak that he no longer hopes for survival, cannot stand these discussions. Even if he should be taken out of Leningrad, he wouldn't survive the trip. Here, sustained by his wife's concern, he can still hang on.

Today after supper came the word that Tikhvin

has been liberated. That means that there is an open road to Vologda. New chances for salvation.

JANUARY 30

My uncle died at four. My aunt opened the casement and went out into the kitchen. Since he was sleeping, she decided to leave him alone and let him sleep a little more. But in half an hour, when she stopped to look in, he was already dead. He lay in his usual peaceful pose. We carried him into the cold room. My aunt, who always adored him, behaved as every-one does now—she didn't even cry. At six in the evening, Ludmilla came home from work. I opened the door for her and told her the sad news of her father's death. Ludmilla wept bitterly and only then, somehow, did it really strike my aunt. She embraced her daughter and wept for a long time in her arms. It was easier to watch this outburst of grief than the terrible hardness which one finds in everyone in Leningrad these days.

FEBRUARY 3

My little Yura is beginning to be covered with boils. There is even a boil on every finger. We tried to lance them, but new ones appear. He looks bad. But worse, are the signs of apathy. I fear that more than anything. Until lately he was the only one in the house who was cheerful and gay. He puttered around in the courtyard, cleared snow, swept pathways, cut wood, but now he clings close to the stove. I am seized by a terrible anxiety. My elder son will die in the hospital and now the same danger threatens my little one.

Doctors say that many men died this winter. By

spring, the women will begin to die out. Women are generally hardier. They have a greater supply of fat under their skin. However, they have begun to fail, too. I myself notice that one of my cheeks is thicker than the other. My body is like a skeleton. Blue veins stand out on my hands. My feet are swollen. I move with great difficulty. If I should fail the whole family will perish. Who would bring these pathetic bread rations on which our lives depend?

FEBRUARY 4

Last night, late, there was a knock at the front door. A man in a sheepskin coat with various military decorations in the buttonholes asked for me. He came for some documents necessary for evacuation. While I looked for the invaluable papers, he followed me with a flashlight. Slowly I turned my attention to his full, well-tended face . . . literally a man from another world who accidentally came across our planet. But he is also surviving the siege of Leningrad. For the hundredth time you reflect on how different can be the situation of people who have power or advantages from that of ordinary people who have nothing but their bread ration cards. Our visitor took our papers and left. He told us that tomorrow we must evacuate.

FEBRUARY 5

A day of insane flurry has ended. The final packing took place in complete darkness. I don't know what I took, what I have forgotten. We are so tired, we can hardly move. My mother, emaciated and with frightening signs of death on her face, also bustled about all day, packing this and that as if she were going to the country. My husband drove to the hospital to get Dima. I had hoped to see the boy a little improved at least, but I was gravely mistaken. Several days ago, Dima came down with dystrophy, a severe stomach ailment which now rages in our city; but despite Dima's grave condition, the head doctor at the hospital nevertheless advised me to take him with us since there is little hope for improvement in Leningrad. With the aid of a chauffeur, my husband carried Dima into our apartment.

And so tomorrow we are leaving. Our party—my seventy-four-year-old, terribly weak mother; our sixty-five-year-old nana, feet swollen, covered with boils, strength undermined by the harsh winter; gravely ill Dima who cannot walk by himself; little Yura, covered with sores, and me. Me—just barely able bodied. I am already beginning to swell. I have especially weakened in these last few days.

The future frightens me. Where will we go and what will happen to us? My aunt, who is also supposed to evacuate with her daughter and grandchildren after her husband's burial, sighs heavily when she looks at me. I know that she doubts the success of this venture. But we will see. There is nothing we can do. There is no other way out.

Friends came to say good-bye today. Will I ever see them again? It is terrible to look at Irina, Yura's godmother, who was so convinced that no one would go hungry. She is all swollen. Her once beautiful face has turned into a transparent mask. Hunger changes the appearance of all. Everyone now is blue-black, bloodless, swollen. If someone had tried makeup to appear to be dying of hunger, he could not come up with such faces. Besides Irina, my other friend, Jennie, horrifies me. Jennie, who only a few months ago, was radiant and beautiful. Nothing of her former beauty remains. She always ate very little, but now she eyes every little piece hungrily. Another friend, also named Irina, and her husband, Igor, barely got here. Not long ago they were healthy, lively sportsmen; now they are old. Luckily, I had some oats, which I won't take with me. From these oats I made a last treat for my guests. How greedily all eyes were glued to that large pot full of steaming liquid. I remembered how almost exactly one year ago, on February 13, on my birthday, all these people had gathered at my home for the traditional supper. How many delicious things there were to eat . . . and so many wines. And after supper—dancing and gaiety until morning. And all that was only a year ago. Ours is a gathering of ghosts.

Exodus

February 6 to May 2, 1942

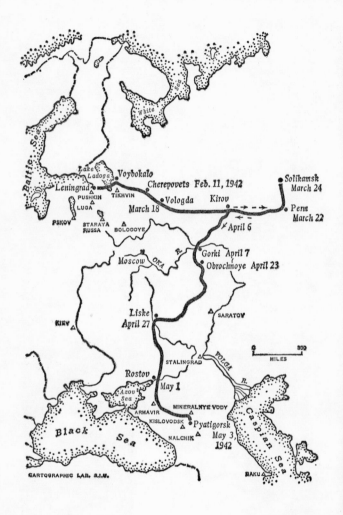

FEBRUARY 11

Yesterday we got off at the Cherepovets station at ten in the morning. It was cold and snowing very hard. We had nowhere to go. I took my mother to the nearest aid station.

And so Leningrad is behind us. But first I must establish these past few days in my memory. I got up quite early on the sixth. It was still dark. Since the beginning of the war I have awakened quite early every morning, but with a feeling of grief and despair. This morning I was hopeful and even happy. First I ran to the bakery to get some bread for the trip. On the way back I stopped, as usual, by the room of our former landlady, Anastasia Vladimirovna, to bring her some bread and a meal. Although the room was completely dark, I could see, stooping over the old woman, that she was dead. I remembered how afraid she had been that we would leave her. Last night, after learning that we were to evacuate, she became despairing. Obviously this blow was too much for her. But really, who would have continued to bring her these crumbs which sustained life in her frail body? Who needs a half-corpse when, all around, healthy, young people are dying? Maybe she realized all this and lost her will to live.

So as not to delay the car, we had to carry our things over at dawn. The departure was set for eight o'clock.

A bright, crisp morning. Frost-covered trees glittered in the sun in front of our house. There was not a cloud in the blue sky. I loved days like this. Days when frost bites at your cheeks, and the sun and snow blind your eyes. But now it was not like that. With difficulty we settled the elderly women in the vehicle. It was even harder with Dima. There was already one family in the car—the mother of a soldier and his wife and child. We still had to drive to the hospital on Kirochnaya where the rest of the evacuees were gathered. Only three cars for thirty people. We waited for a long time . . . at least three hours. The hospital director's family was late. The others claimed that they probably had not had enough time to pack all their things. Finally a robust, glowing woman appeared, elegantly and warmly dressed. With her were two well-fed girls about twelve or thirteen years of age, and besides them, another little girl with her governess. The strict laws of evacuation do not exist for such families. It is just we poor mortals who are not allowed to take friends with us. Later there were some other people who changed seats and cars. They also squeezed some huge tanks into our car, which left us no room in which to turn around. The tanks were filled with gasoline, and the air became heavy with the smell. Of course our leaders picked out the best car for themselves, while ours, which had some defect or another, was to lumber along between two others. Although I had little interest in those around me, in spite of myself, I could only notice that the families of hospital employees look wonderful. In our car there was a fat little boy, the son of an official of the hospital. Next to my Dima, he seems especially rosy and healthy, and Dima looks deathly.

Finally everything was ready. Last farewells. I watched my husband and the young soldier, whose family was in the car, strain their remaining strength to run after us. Too soon they were out of sight.

The city flashed by us—all those sections with which the happiest years of my life are tied. We passed Znamenskaya and drove back over Kirochnaya, getting a final glimpse of our house . . . Tavrichevski garden where I played as a child . . . farther, the Pedagogical Institute where I studied. We passed Smolni, then familiar suburbs, country places where we often went on Sundays in overcrowded trains.

Dima leaned on me more and more heavily. He is worse. I gave him swallows of wine from a bottle, tried to cheer him and convince him that soon we will be out of the ring, that we will go south, which he so yearned for, that he will get better, go to school again and have everything. I tell him these things, but I don't believe them myself.

We drove to Lake Ladoga and there our trials began. Something was not right with the car; it stopped altogether. Everyone passed by us. The car that was supposed to follow us and render aid when necessary, went ahead. We were left alone on the endless, snowy plain. The chauffeur and his helper struggled with the repairs. It got colder. Near us rushed an endless stream of cars. Everyone wants to get across such dangerous places as Lake Ladoga which is subject to continuous bombing and artillery fire, as soon as possible. Dusk. There was not even a trace of the two other cars. And our car stalled every five minutes. We were really beginning to freeze. In order to heat up the little stove, we would have had to drag out the gas tanks, and that could have caused an explosion. Everything is always so complicated, difficult, and exhausting.

It was not until ten P.M. that we got to the opposite shore. We had hoped that the other cars would be waiting for us. But they were gone. Our bad situation was intensified by the fact that no one knew at which station we were to meet the train or where we could find the people responsible for the evacuation. Our drivers managed to spend the night in a hut, while we had to sleep in the car in various twisted poses. That was an endless, wearisome night. Finally—dawn. I decided to take the initiative. I insisted that we go to Voybokalo where there is an infirmary for whose director I had a letter.

We had just started off when an alarm sounded. German planes flew over us. Antiaircraft guns pounded at them. After a few versts, we came upon the two cars with which we had left Leningrad. The hospital director showered us with reproaches for lagging behind. But the next day I learned accidentally that the officials had celebrated all night with the food designated for the whole transport. Of course they were little touched by the fact that the car carrying a dying boy had broken down. The only measure which our leader took was to take his son out of our car and into his. I couldn't stand it any longer. How could they leave the gravely ill Dima in such an unreliable car? My fellow passengers supported my complaint. Finally, Dima was transferred to the other car to be taken to the infirmary in Voybokalo.

Later I saw that infirmary—scores of tents scattered over a snow-covered field. I had to leave Dima there, however, because his condition has gotten so much worse. I said good-bye and gave him his passport. The official who now had charge of our car was in a hurry. I could not linger, as our train was to leave any moment.

So here I am in a railway car with my old ones and Yura. There was not one vacant spot. We sat on our suitcases. Besides that discomfort, there was torture of another order. In the morning the wife of the evacuating hospital director and her daughters took out some fried chickens, chocolate, and condensed milk, at the sight of which, Yura fainted. My throat was seized by spasms, but not from hunger. . . .

Toward dinner time, this family showed its "tact." They curtained off their corner and we no longer had to look at people eating chicken, pirozhki (meat cakes), and butter. It is hard to remain silent because of indignation and anger. But to whom could I have complained? I kept quiet. Besides, we are used to this after so many years.

Travel by night is worse than by day. My hands have swollen. I had to hold Yura on my lap all night. It never occurred to anyone to give up his seat for a while. My mother and nana were also very tired. And in addition, someone beat on the doors with a hammer at every stop. I don't know who—trainmen or orderlies. They pounded deafeningly on the walls and shouted, "Do you have any dead? Hand them over to us."

FEBRUARY 12

I didn't have the chance to write down everything yesterday. I was so exhausted. Today I am still very tired. I was in turmoil all day. In vain I had thought that it would be enough to break out of the blockade. Then life would be easier. I have come to the conclusion that it is the same all over—starvation, destruction, disease, and death. There is nothing. Just as if people had eaten up all their supplies in half a year. Yura asks me, "Did their warehouses burn down, too? Who burned them?" I can find no answers either for his questions or my own.

But I had better continue the story of our journey. The train moved slowly, spending hours at stations and substations. During these stops, supper and bread were given out to the long lines, supper being soup and porridge. True, the first day they did distribute some sausage. However, my travelmates found a way to steal it from me. Sitting all night with Yura in my arms, I could not keep track of my things.

Stomach ailments have begun to plague our trip. Probably because people are so unaccustomed to food.

Startlingly, the majority of the passengers in our railway car, representatives of the intelligentsia, behaved in a most heartless manner. At one stop our nana got out of the car, was delayed, and got back just as the train was pulling out again. Some of the passengers had to help her get back in. This insignificant incident caused everyone present to jump at me with the complaint that I do not watch after my own. I didn't have the strength to argue with that horde of malicious people. The loudest protestors were those with the largest food supply.

On the fourth day I decided to get out at the first, best stop—just to put an end to the murderous journey. We reached Cherepovets. There I have neither relatives nor friends. But among the travelers there was one, Gavrilova, whom I knew slightly in Leningrad and who told me that she had many friends in Cherepovets. She said she would talk to them and that they would help us to find a place and a means by which to stay. I realized that it was absolutely vital to stop. My mother could go no further. She weakens with every hour. She has lost strength because of all those sleepless nights. Besides this, I am tortured by the thought of Dima. Maybe from here I can get to him at the hospital.

And so we are on the platform of the train station. A gray sky hangs over our heads. Snow is falling. Our breath is short from the intense cold. I was much relieved when I was able to leave my mother at an overcrowded, filthy aid station. I was so afraid that she would not survive the terrible journey and that at some stop or another, at the usual question, "Do you have any dead?" the other passengers would hand over my mother. At the moment, this repulsive aid station seems like a godsend.

Gavrilova went into town to find her friends. We stood around our belongings. Local citizens would come up to us to express their surprise at our stopping in Cherepovets. They told us that rampant starvation has spread throughout the town and surrounding countryside. Gavrilova finally appeared. She told us that there was a small room for us. We set off along the dark narrow streets of the city's outskirts. Our hosts greeted us glumly. Here they fear Leningraders most of all because they are all sick and hungry. There could not even be any talk about help from the local establishment. One of these is our host, whose pantry is filled with food. I think about such popular terms as "our people" and "strangers." Right now I am more worried that Yura won't be able to stand it and will ask our hosts for a piece of bread.

Stopping in Cherepovets has done us no good. The food situation here is very bad. The people are given 400 grams of bread and that's all. Of course, for the local citizens this is still not tragic, because they have their gardens and can rely on potatoes and vegetables to some extent. But refugees find it hard to exist, especially since there are so many in Cherepovets. Evacuees stop here as we did, some partly because of the illness of some member of the family. The supervising officer in charge of evacuees told me curtly and bluntly to leave as soon as possible. He will not continue our rations any longer than for three days. No one is allowed to register in Cherepovets unless he has relatives here.

I run about from morning until night, knocking on every door. The first problem is to get permission to stay in Cherepovets for at least two more weeks, so that my mother and nana might get back some strength to go with us to the Caucasus. The second problem is to get permission to go to Voybokalo to Dima. I am still hoping that he has improved. But all my attempts have brought no results. I was refused everywhere. They won't even give me permission to stay for a short time; many people are dying in the city. The head of the NKVD * to whom

---

* *NKVD stands for the People's Commission for Internal Affairs, or the Russian secret police. Many enterprises, prison camps, and mines were administered directly by this*

I turned with my Voybokalo request categorically announced that the civilian population is not allowed passage to the front zone under any circumstances.

FEBRUARY 17

I took my mother out of the aid station. She gets weaker with every hour. Nana can also barely walk. I have nothing to give them. Everyone tells me to put them in a hospital. I went to a doctor and asked him to make a house call. He promised he would come tomorrow. We will see what he advises.

FEBRUARY 18

Today they took the elderly women to the hospital. Of course, this is a hospital in name only. In all my life I have never seen such an institution: unbelievable filth, no bed linen, unbearable stench and no care for the patients.

Last night, returning from the city mess hall where we stood in line nearly all day for soup and coffee, Yura and I got lost. Our route lies past a church and cemetery, crossing which, we enter into vacant land. Later the suburb streets, on one of which we live, start again.

Evidently I lost the way. We walked for a long time but there were no street signs. Yura was tired, and his legs barely cleared snowbanks. He asked me constantly, "Where are we?" I became frightened. Not one soul was near us. No one to tell us where we were. We turned right, then left. We wandered for more than two hours until, finally, we met an old

---

agency. The NKVD had its own special military forces as well [ED.].

woman who showed us the way. It was like a dreary fairy tale I might have read as a child: a poor wretch walking over a strange landscape, forest and wild animals all around him, above him a star-strewn sky; he lifts his eyes to heaven, whispers a prayer and plods onward.

Starving, dying Leningrad is behind us. Yura and I are lost in a strange town. Thoughts about Dima's fate and my concern over the ill elderly women give me no peace. Added to all that, the mocking, heartless attitude of people in whose hands our own fates lie today: those people who control the bread ration, a plate of soup, a corner to sleep in. There are times when you just want to fold your hands and forget about everything—let be what will be. But man is made differently. Despite all these trials and with his last strength, he will strive to catch at a straw. My motivation is my children.

FEBRUARY 20

I visit my mother and nana every day. And every day new half-dead Leningraders are taken off trains and brought to the hospital. Each morning, wide country rigs loaded with corpses block the door of the hospital. They take the dead straight to a field and bury them in a common grave without markers or funeral services. Today I saw a young woman, perhaps twenty years old, near the hospital entrance. She sat on the snow. Tears froze to her cheeks. Her husband, a student, died during the night. They had been married for less than a year, and starved in Leningrad, but managed to evacuate together. Along the way they were taken off the train and sent to this hospital. The husband, in especially bad condition, was to be kept longer, but he died. Later I met another young couple. He is an engineer and she is a student. They were also taken off the train because they were so weak. They hope to gain strength and push farther south.

FEBRUARY 21

When I come to the hospital my mother and nana must first tell me everything that has occurred during the night. Today they told me that the young pair I had met, died. They died at nearly the same moment. And four young girls—students—who had been brought to the hospital just that evening, also died. There was no room, so they were put on the floor in the hall, and by dawn they were four corpses.

My mother is getting worse and worse. She had a little too much milk to drink, and in her condition that could be fatal—terrible stomach ailment. That is just what Zoya Tarnovskaya died of a month ago.

I turned my attention to the fact that the hospital is full of sick people, the majority of whom are intelligent people—engineers, teachers, students—and yet not one among them cares what is going on at the front. Maybe thoughts about their personal fates or the stupor brought on by starvation has caused this loss of interest in everything that is going on beyond the confines of the hospital.

FEBRUARY 23

There was no hope for any kind of help. It was just as if Yura and I found ourselves in a barren, snow-ridden wasteland—and suddenly, an oasis. Running from one building to another, I accidently ended up at the evacuation center. In the room were three people—two doctors, one, a woman, and a young typist-secretary. To my amazement these people received me very pleasantly. They asked questions and promised to help me find Dima. They took my letters to be sent to his hospital and wrote their own concerning his whereabouts if he should no longer be there. Of course they couldn't do much, especially since there are strict laws concerning the disposition of refugees and their further evacuation. But nevertheless, the kind words and extremely sincere concern made me feel better.

There is nothing but cranberries at the marketplace now. I buy them and we eat them along with baked potatoes. I take this treat to the hospital too, since the food there is unfit. I managed to get the potatoes from a peasant woman in exchange for a piece of woolen material.

FEBRUARY 25

I write letters endlessly to all my friends whose addresses I managed to save. I send telegrams. But I get no answers. I might as well have thrown all my messages into a bottomless well. I feel cut off from the rest of the world. I think Robinson Crusoe was a lucky man. He knew quite well that he was on an uninhabited island and that he had to rely only on himself. But I am among people.

I petition constantly for leave to go to Vologda where I hope to find Dima. My mother is in no condition to travel any farther. The doctor tells me that her heart is good, but I am afraid that she won't improve. A few days ago a transport left for the Caucasus. I begged the director of refugee affairs to get us on it, but he refused. He said this transport was a private one. Later, on the side, I learned that it was designated for employees of the NKVD and left only half-full. But I have gotten used to such wrongs and the realization that even in such times, distinctions among people still prevail.

FEBRUARY 26

The coldness shown us by those on whom our fate depends, to some extent, has had a favorable result. Thanks to all these denials and my mother's stay in the hospital, I have received, although with interruption, an extension of our bread rations. We have been in Cherepovets for two weeks already. It is hard, but Yura and I have managed to get along.

During this time I have been able to observe life in this little town. Lord knows what is going on. It turns out that the more prominent officials hold banquets regularly once a week, if not more often. What they don't do at these parties! And all of it out of the funds assigned for starving Leningrad refugees. The town is very small, so anything that happens is immediately common knowledge. I found this all out from a girl who lives with Gavrilova. The girl takes advantage of the supply manager's affections and attends the parties he gives. She says that the table is always full of every kind of food. There is plenty of it, and wine flows in rivers.

FEBRUARY 26, *night*

I awoke from some unexplainable uneasiness. I can't sleep. I turned on the lamp. Even the usual problems do not trouble me as much as this undefinable foreboding. I am very disturbed. It is a good thing that

Yura is sleeping so soundly. He has not even moved while I have been writing.

FEBRUARY 27

I went to the hospital sooner than usual—at ten. I found my mother dead. She died near morning. Nana, whose cot stands nearby, told me that she died peacefully. But she was only trying to cheer me up, because another neighbor confided that my mother had tossed violently before she died. And this is how it must have been. My mother's hands are twisted, her mouth, contorted. She is so changed that, looking at her, I can't believe this is my mother who was always so beautiful. I stood at her bed for a long time. I cried hard. My conscience troubles me that I could not save her and that I could have made her last days happier. I was so busy with getting our daily dole and with saving the children, that I did not give her enough attention. Now I can't even bury her properly. No one will volunteer to dig a separate grave. All corpses are dumped in common graves. These are called "Leningradian." Many are buried this way, young and old—men, women, and children who left Leningrad but couldn't be saved from starvation. While I stood there, they came for my mother. Indifferent people take away the corpses and toss them in a common heap. Yura waits for me outside the hospital and plays in the snow. Lately, the color has come back to his cheeks. Only he makes me realize that I must go on. That there is still a reason to live, that I must fight to escape that death which has already swallowed so many victims.

FEBRUARY 28

There is only one thing to do—wait until Nana gets out of the hospital (she has gotten better) and leave as soon as possible, to get away from this place which has caused so much pain and grief.

And besides grief—all the humiliations—even the difficulty of continuing our ration cards. I wouldn't wish my worst enemy to live through what I have had to during these five weeks in Cherepovets. We are still lucky that one of the staff of the city management office has taken pity on my hopeless situation and continues to write out tickets for bread and dinner. But each time I come, she tries to persuade me to leave quickly. I can understand her. She is afraid. It will go badly for her if her superior should learn of her action.

MARCH 3

Nana has left the hospital. But she is still weak and can hardly walk. I don't know how I can take her any farther. There is no news from Dima. I got a notice from the Voybokalo hospital that Dima was one of those evacuated. The ill were shipped east, but just where, was not made clear. At the evacuation center I learned that the especially weak have been left in various hospitals along the way.

So guess. The way the infirmaries and hospitals are organized, it is impossible to locate anyone. I can only hope that if the boy has improved, then perhaps he will make his way to Ivanovo-Voznesensk. We have relatives there. They will take care of him.

MARCH 5

I go to the train station all the time, trying to get us on the transport coming out of Leningrad. However, so far there is no hope. All of them are extremely crowded. They can take no one from Cherepovets. But we must get out of here. And soon. This matter of the bread ration has become life or death. If that kind girl should discontinue our rations, which she has every right to do at any time, then we will die of starvation here in Cherepovets. There is positively nothing to buy or trade for at the marketplace. I can trade our rationed bread for milk, which is so necessary for Yura. For a long time now, we have not received any dinner. Only the bread keeps us alive.

A few days ago, Gavrilova and I went about ten versts into the country.* We hoped to trade some things for food. We returned empty-handed. Peasants chase such as us away. They need nothing more, especially since they garnered a lot of things earlier: rugs, various piecegoods, etc. After this humiliation, I promised myself never to try it again. It hurts too much to feel like a beggar, pleading for a crumb of bread.

MARCH 7

Your heart warms whenever you meet with even the smallest favor. Our cool host has thawed a little. In the evenings he invites us to sit with him by the

* *One verst equals 3500 feet, just about the same as a kilometer* [ED.].

samovar. Of course all we can count on is a cup of boiling water, but thank God for that. It is twice as heart-warming—from the water and from our host's sympathy.

MARCH 10

A telegram came from my aunt in Siberia today. I had written her of my mother's death. She asks how she can help. And just how can she help when she is in Siberia and we are in Cherepovets?

I tried to search out an acquaintance who had been a friend of my husband. I know that now he holds an important position. I found him and asked for help. But he cannot offer us any. Perhaps he doesn't want to.

MARCH 12

Today I went to the post office to send telegrams off in all directions. For some reason I decided to ask for my mail. What was my amazement when I was handed a small note from Dima! It turns out that he is no longer at the field hospital I left him in, but in Tikhvin, by his reckoning. He didn't get any of my letters. Afraid for us and for himself, he wrote to all those towns which might have been along our route. I had once mentioned Cherepovets as a possible place where we could try to stay until spring. Dima's letter was despairing. "Mother, where are you?" it began. "I don't know what to do. Any day they might release me, though I am still very weak. Where should I go, without things, money, or an evacuee's ration card for bread?" The rest of the letter was along that line. I wired him some money, a telegram, and sent him a letter. Afterward I ran to all the offices again, in the hope that on the basis of Dima's letter, I might get permission to go after him. Tikhvin is only a two hour's ride from Cherepovets. I was refused everywhere. Tikhvin—near the front, off-limits area, passage forbidden.

MARCH 15

Be what may, I have decided to leave. Today. Of course there are no prospects for any such possibility. But what can I do? I am going to take Yura and nana to the train station. It is not possible to stay here any longer. We will get absolutely no more bread. And there can't even be any talk of registering ourselves here. I tried that before.

If Dima got even one of my letters, and he finds out that we are in Cherepovets, he will certainly come here. I begged the doctors at the evacuation center to help him if he should suddenly appear.

MARCH 17

In front of me, there's a picture window. Behind it floats a pine forest. I look at this forest, at the snow-banks, at the sky, and I can't believe that it's all real. I am sitting at a table on which there's a typewriter, my typewriter, carried out of Leningrad and which I will finally use now.* But I can't get used to the thought that all this has really happened, that it's not a dream.

But to put everything in order. Just as I had decided on the fifteenth of March, I settled matters

* *Thanks to a neighbor, Victor, my typewriter was fixed in late November* [AUTHOR].

with my landlord and got a sleigh on which to pile
all our things. We trudged along in the snow behind
the sleigh, Yura, nana, and I. Later, Gavrilova
caught up with us. At the last minute she decided to
throw her lot in with ours. And so we got to the railroad station. There they told us that not one transport was expected. There had been a severe blizzard
and the tracks were buried under many feet of snow.
But we stayed at the station and settled ourselves
somehow on our belongings. We waited until ten
that evening. And suddenly, unexpectedly, an evacuee train emerged from the storm. I begged the commander of the train to take us. He was sympathetic
but warned us that the train was packed with trade
apprentices who were utterly disorganized. They
were capable of tearing our belongings apart and taking away what little food we had. In general he advised me to wait until the next day. There was nothing to do. We decided to return to the city to spend
the night and begin all over again in the morning.
This we did. We went to some of Gavrilova's friends
and spent the night on the cold floor since there
weren't enough beds for unexpected guests. In the
morning we went to the station again. As we approached, we saw that two trains stood on the tracks.
One—a hospital train, an enormous, spotless, new car
with sealed doors. The other, filled with evacuating,
exhausted, grimy people. It turned out that one of
the cars in the transport was reserved for passengers
from Cherepovets. So we had to scramble into that
one. But all around teemed other anxious evacuees.
Women with packages and trunks, bundles, cradles,
and other treasures climbed onto the train. They
yelled, screamed, and pushed at each other. I don't
know how I got the strength to get through and some-

how squeeze our things and ourselves onto the train. Someone hit nana on the head with a trunk. The poor woman was nearly unconscious. Yura began to scream and cry in terror. He desperately wanted to get out of that terrible place. I couldn't stand it. I started to throw our things out of the train onto the platform. We eased out after them. With us, Gavrilova. She was seething. She decided that I had completely lost my mind. But she did not stay in the train. And so here we were again in a heap on the platform. Gavrilova insisted that I find the director of the station. But I couldn't grasp anything at the moment. I don't know how, but I began telling my woes to Red Army soldiers from the hospital train which stood nearby. And then one of them, an elderly, mustachioed soldier began to question me concerning where I had left Dima. He told me that in the train was a young boy who looked to be about fifteen years old but that he was very weak. I had a fleeting moment of insane hope—perhaps it was Dima. I clambered onto the car the soldier had pointed out. Yura ran along, grasping my hand tightly. Looking at us, the soldier jumped into the train. I stood on the footboard, neither alive nor dead. Perhaps a minute passed when Dima appeared in the doorway, pale, swollen, extremely weak, but alive. He was helped down the steps where I could embrace him. He could barely stand up. This scene touched the onlookers. The crowd around us grew. I thanked the soldier who had brought us to the train. But he waved us away and advised, "Try the train commander. We will still be here a few more minutes." If he hadn't said anything, I wouldn't have even thought of asking for a place on that shining, compartmented hospital train. I had thought those salons were unattainable. But I rushed to the staff car and found the chief doctor immediately. Tripping over every word, I told him my troubles. "Wait a minute," he said and left hurriedly. And in a minute or two he was back, telling me to hurry and get into the hospital train. I ran ahead, calling nana, and begged people standing on the platform to help us load our things. Here Gavrilova abruptly changed her manner. Her anger vanished completely. We just managed to grab our belongings and put them into the baggage car, when our train started off.

I had barely come to myself when I sat down by this wide, picture window, that same window at which I am now writing. I saw Cherepovets being left behind. How much we suffered in that town where we lived for a month and six days. Those days could have become eternity. It is hard to describe the happy relief I feel now that we are leaving this unfortunate town. And at the same time, grief that here, in a common grave, lies my mother.

MARCH 18

This morning is rich with happy moments. Above all, we slept well . . . the first time in many anxious days and nights. I went to the train commander to find out how far he will let us ride. When he learned that the next big stop, Vologda, would not help us, he suggested we go farther. "We can take you to Baikal." To formalize our passage in the train, he asked that I work as a typist, especially since I have a typewriter with me. In half an hour I was sitting in the staff office with certain communiqués to be typed up, lying in front of me. My swollen fingers miss the keys. The last time I typed was several months ago. I hope the swelling will go down and my fingers will become more flexible. Most of all, it seems that the humiliation of begging for bread has ended. I am definitely a member of the train staff. Even Yura, for the first time in his life, is registered according to the law; in order that his ration will be guaranteed, he is included among the number of orderlies. Of course, his age is not noted. And he is not quite six years old yet.

We are saved. As I write these lines, the train is passing Vologda. We are going onward to Perm. Fields, forests, and villages, all snow-laden, flash by me. The train is carrying us farther. Behind us—air raids, artillery, starvation, darkness, and death.

MARCH 19

And thus we are now employees of the hospital train, and apparently we are heading for Siberia. Dima told me about his adventures in Cherepovets. He had somehow received one of my numerous letters and had learned of our whereabouts. He gave this information to the hospital director, who decided to send him as far as Cherepovets with the first hospital train going toward the interior of the country. That hospital train arrived at Cherepovets late in the evening, having taken four days to go from Tikhvin to Cherepovets. Dima thanked the train commander and took leave of the crew who had all been informed about the boy looking for this mother and who had been very nice to him. He then headed for the address which he had. What a disappointment it was for him when he found out from my landlords that Yura and I had just left Cherepovets that very day. The landlord, nonetheless, gave Dima the money and things that I had left behind in any case for him and he sadly headed back to the station. Fortunately for him his train had not yet left, and the commander, Dmitri Aleksandrovich, agreed to take him further to the rear, at least to Vologda. At that very same time we were still in Cherepovets, spending the night with Gavrilova's landlady. Going to the station in the morning, we did not find out anything about what had taken place. The mere chance that we met each other was Dima's salvation. He was still so weak that he never could have overcome all the difficulties alone. He would not have been taken in by any military hospital since he was not a soldier.

The train commander summoned me and asked me about my plans. I showed him the evacuation document with Pyatigorsk as the destination. This train, however, was headed for Siberia. Dmitri Aleksandrovich reflected a while not knowing how to act toward us. He decided to allow us to go to Vologda for the time being, and there we would see what would be. All the same, it was still further into the heart of the country.

MARCH 19

We are going very slowly. At every station there are extended stops. I am extremely happy about that. The thought of our again being without a roof and without food frightens me. Dima and especially nana are still very weak. Dima, Yura, and I are receiving rations, which are so large that we cannot eat them all and we share them with nana and Gavrilova. I scarcely see Yurochka since he spends the entire day among the wounded. Everybody fell in love with him and they all talk with him and entertain him. He already knows all their names and considers them his friends. My work begins in the morning and consists of typing military reports for the train commissar. This does not take more than two or three hours a day. At first the commissar did not regard my work with favor since my fingers refused to obey me the first few minutes; they looked more like wooden stumps than like part of the human body, but after an hour I was able to adapt myself and he softened up. From his appearance, tall, fat, with pock-marked face, reddish hair, and small penetrating eyes under hanging brows, this commissar could have frightened anyone. Both he and the NKVD representative, a young, lively, small, even handsome man, but with hostile, cold, gray eyes, frighten me somewhat. The remaining crew of the train, however, especially the train commander and the quartermaster, received us like their own. The train commander transferred Dima from the car for wounded Red Army soldiers to the employees' car in which Yura and I sleep. This was very nice on his part and very convenient for me, since now I go myself to the kitchen to get dinner for all of us. The cook is an extremely nice Ukrainian, who is apparently touched by our fate, and he helps me in every way possible to feed Dima.

MARCH 20

We have been allowed to continue the trip with the hospital train past Vologda. The commissar whom I feared so much the first few days, gave a good report about my work. Also we apparently do not bother the NKVD representative by our presence. He does not even notice us since he is all bound up in his romance with a pretty nurse. I believe she is a good influence on him since she is very attached to Yura, who reminds her of her little brother and during her free hours—free from work and love—she takes Yura through the cars of wounded and plays with him. She is always in a good mood. It is strange on what a person's fate can depend!

Because of the decision of the train commander to allow us to remain on the train until Siberia I am changing my plans. Now I think that the best thing for us would be to go to my cousin who is now established in his specialty in Siberia, to which he came after his evacuation from Moscow several months ago. The main reason for this decision is my desire not to get separated from the crew of this hospital train. Our relationship with all these people is so different from all that we have had to experience during our wandering, that I simply am afraid of losing them.

MARCH 22

Today, having awakened early, I overheard the conversation of two young nurses who were sleeping in the same compartment as we. They were talking about some type of new orders, received last evening. The train's direction has been changed. Instead of Siberia, we are now heading north to Solikamsk. It seems that there they are supposed to unload all the wounded; that means us too; and the train will go back to the front for a new load. I immediately went to the commander to find out from him personally about the change in itinerary and about our fate in this connection. Dmitri Aleksandrovich confirmed the conversation I had overheard. In Solikamsk he was to unload the entire train; one crew was to remain. I told him that I did not have a single acquaintance in that city, and that I was frightened by the thought of again being with the children and the old nana in such a remote, northern cold city. The commander, having discussed our situation with the commissar, promised to take us back to Perm, and then we could decide further. This was a wonderful way out of the dilemma. First, we could stay at least another week on the train, and this under present conditions is already a lot. In addition, we will then again be on the main track going to Siberia and to the Caucasus. There could be no chance of remaining any longer on the hospital train since after delivering the wounded, the train has to return quickly to the Leningrad front. Doctor Kazakov explained to me that hospital trains also underwent shelling and bombing. On many occasions already he had had to rush from the train and seek shelter from bombs in the nearest ditch, in the woods, and sometimes simply lie in the open field. His most convincing argument influencing my decision was his statement that, "You should not risk having your children killed before your eyes."

MARCH 23

We are traveling along the Urals to the north. I sit for hours near the huge picture window of the staff car, where my office is now established and I admire the unusual, beautiful, grim, northern landscape of Russia. I had heard much about the beauty of the Ural area, but this was the first time I had seen it. Tomorrow we should be in Solikamsk. Yura is already sad about the fact that he will have to part with all his friends, the wounded. Yesterday evening, the quartermaster officer, a very fine fellow who spoils

Yura terribly, allowed him to play the part of the train officer on duty. You should have seen Yura with an officer's cap down to his ears and a pistol holster at his belt marching along the corridor of the staff car with an unbelievably serious expression on his face. The whole command, including the commissar and train commander, observed this picture holding back a smile. This helped Yura's self-assurance even more and he was now convinced that he was indeed a genuine officer of the guard fulfilling his duties.

MARCH 24

All morning the wounded were being unloaded. During the eight days of the trip we had come to know them so well that separating was extremely difficult. We had regained our strength and were like new born. Under these favorable conditions we are reacting entirely differently than two months ago in starving Leningrad when we stepped over corpses with indifference. The hardness and indifference, peculiarities of all Leningraders at that time, has now disappeared. Yura simply sobbed when they carried all his friends out on stretchers. I too was unusually sad knowing full well that these boys are far from the last. How many more victims will this war bring!

MARCH 26

We are returning with an empty train. The crew and the five of us. Dima has recovered so well during this time that it's hard to recognize him. It is as though he had been to a health resort. As before the train often sits at the stations. One has the impression that no one is hurrying. Quite frankly I am amazed; indeed, everyone knows what a shortage of transportation we have. At the stops we are permitted to go into the woods to the nearest villages. Almost every day the crew is busy with all types of military training exercises. To Yura's great joy they take him with them. Returning from these exercises, he is so ruddy, fresh, and healthy, that it is difficult to imagine that this is the very boy who, such a short time ago, pale and weak, had apathetically ceased to react to life.

MARCH 27

Today we took our trip to the village and there we exchanged various things for a leg of veal. The peasants here are not as spoiled as the ones near Leningrad and they are very eager for all articles of clothing of which there is a tremendous shortage. By this cold (it is now more than 40 below) many cannot even go out on the street since they have no warm clothing or footwear. Thus a pair of valenki (felt boots) here is worth its weight in gold. Upon our return, the veal was given to the cook and he arranged a real feast, adding all the necessary accoutrements in the form of potatoes and vegetables. The entire crew was invited.

In our compartment there are three girls with the rank of lieutenant. For whole days now they play the guitar and sing songs. We are traveling in gay spirits. However, my nana got involved in an incident that almost resulted in our NKVD agent putting her off the train. She decided to tell fortunes by cards. Of course all the youthful crew crowded around her with great interest and did not notice Danilov passing by. The latter was enraged and threatened to put her off the train. The poor woman was frightened to death. She hid her cards and is sitting neither dead nor alive. Especially unpleasant for her is the fact that she has been deprived of those gifts with which her admirers rewarded her talent. Our girls also are unhappy, not hearing any more stories about the secret King of Clubs and the forthcoming meeting with him or about the jealous rival and the victory over her.

APRIL 1

The train is again approaching Perm. I told the commander that my cousin Marina and her son, who had evacuated with the Hermitage from Leningrad at the beginning of the war, were now living not far from here. He suggested that I should look for them since the train would be delayed in Perm for several days. I would like very much to see Marina and speak with her and maybe even remain here with her. However, this feeling is superseded by the fear of missing the train and our friends with whom we have spent more than two weeks. Today Dmitri Aleksandrovich told me that he and his co-workers would not object if we remain on the train a little longer, this despite the possibility of some unpleasantness in the event of an inspection which now and then takes place on such trains. Nonetheless, he considers that the most important question for us is the one about which he spoke to me earlier—the danger from bombing and shelling. I have still other doubts. We have to help nana get through to her home in the Gorki region, where she is hoping to stay until the end of the war. The second question worrying me is what to do with Yura. He has gotten entirely out of hand, surrounded by so much love and attention. There are times when

the train moves and he is not even in the car. He
rushes out of the car at the stops without asking anyone. For a child such a life on wheels is not entirely
normal. And finally, the stations and the railroad lines
are especially dirty. Indeed freight trains full of
evacuees are moving without interruption; of course
there are no latrines on these trains and everything
occurs en route, between the cars, and there is no
one to clean up. With the present cold weather this
is not a danger, but what will happen when spring
comes? Doctor Kazakov foresees plenty of disease.

APRIL 6

The whole way from Perm to Kirov I was tortured
by doubts. It would be terrible to leave the hospital
train and all these responsive people who have helped
us so much at such a difficult time. Two days ago in
the morning I was standing in the staff room and
studying the map when Dmitri Aleksandrovich came
up and said: "It is obvious that you are still being
drawn by the Caucasus, but I would advise you to go
to Siberia; there at any rate it will be less dangerous;
go to my family (he was from Krasnoyarsk); they
will take you in and help you." Some type of feeling
told me he was right. More than once I had heard
that people in Siberia are something special, more
hospitable than anywhere else. The country was always rich and the people are more grandiose, less
petty. Besides, I had taken on many letters to relatives and friends, from Dmitri Aleksandrovich, and
from other employees of the train. This train had
been formed in Krasnoyarsk and many of the crew
were natives of Siberia. The thoughts about the
Caucasus prevented me from taking this intelligent

decision. The front was so far from Pyatigorsk that it was somehow even strange to think of danger. The main thing which attracted us all, and especially attracted Dima, was the sun and the warmth. The end of the winter was not in sight. We had been freezing in Leningrad since October. Since December, when all the windows had been knocked out, we had been living as if out on the street. In Cherepovets, during our five-week stay, there had also been severe cold, and now the thought of going to Siberia where warm weather was still far off frightened us. We vacillated terribly. We made the decision early this morning. Quickly we packed the few belongings we had with us; our larger baggage had not been unpacked. The crew helped us transfer our baggage to the other track along which the train to Gorki was supposed to go. Our route to the Caucasus went by way of Gorki. We had to part quickly from our friends, who could not be detained long. They had been granted leave from the hospital train for only half an hour.

When the train to Gorki approached it became clear that we would not be able to fight our way through the thick crowd standing on the platform, on the steps of the cars, in the passageways, and in between the cars. People were sitting and lying even on the roofs and were hanging like grape bunches from the entire train. Seeing our confusion and even despair, some helpful people took our suitcases and tried to push us through, but at that very minute the train began to move. We were pushed off but part of our things remained on the train. Fortunately for us, Yura's best friend, Novoselov, the quartermaster of the hospital train, was returning from Kirov where he had spent the whole day with his sister who was living there. He took the initiative and helped us

check the rest of our baggage in the storage room.
The baggage room was so full that they had not
been taking baggage from civilians for a long time
and all the would-be passengers were sitting on their
things in the square in front of the station under the
rain and snow. We, however, were lodged in a large
bright room over the railroad station where only officers' families could spend the night. With unbelievable difficulty we had made our way through the
crowded mass of people lying on the station floor.
These people were still lucky, however, in comparison with those who were spending the night outside.
We had by chance gotten into the "top circle" of people of our country, the country where they shout so
much about equal rights. This situation of being
among "the elect" was extremely pleasant when I saw
the beds, made up with white linen, and it was especially so when, approaching the window and opening the curtain, I observed what was going on in the
station square. From the April sky, snow mixed with
rain was falling.

APRIL 8

Yesterday at ten o'clock in the evening we arrived in
Gorki safe and sound. The departure from Kirov had
not been easy. Knowing already how difficult it was
to get on a train, I promised to give a loaf of bread to
two healthy soldiers in advance. These men had probably not yet been to the Leningrad front and fortunately had no luggage. They were going in the same
direction as we were and they willingly agreed to
aid us. Using their elbows to push aside the people
who were crowding around the car doors, and moving like a flash, they pushed us and our things into

the car almost before we knew what was happening. Thus, we found ourselves on the floor of the overcrowded train. However, this time we all came out together, Gavrilova, nana, Dima, Yura, and I and our somewhat diminished baggage. Everybody was sitting on the floor and even then sitting very crowded since there were no free seats. Even the nets for the baggage were taken by people. Some sort of soldier with a whole chest full of medals immediately took charge of Yura and did not let go of him all the way to Gorki, even giving him a part of his bench where he arranged something in the way of a bed. The car was filled to the brim, and it was difficult to breathe because of the stuffiness. Despite this and although all our joints ached from sitting hunched up and uncomfortable on the floor, I felt happier than I had long ago in peacetime when the international train took me from Leningrad to the seaside resort. How relative everything is. At ten o'clock in the evening of the following day we pulled into Gorki. And here it even smelled of war. The station was darkened to such a degree that nothing was visible. Now began the procedure of checking our things in the baggage room; I was surprised to see that here everything went much easier than in Kirov. Obviously, there are fewer refugees. A man in civilian clothes approached and proposed to lead me to the "room for mothers and children." Here it was incomparably better than in the station, where, as in Kirov, people were sitting and sleeping on the floor. Meanwhile Gavrilova and Dima were busy with transferring our things and nana was watching the remaining items. In the darkness reigning everywhere the guard did not notice her and closed the gate leading out to the platform. The frightened old lady began to call for help. Dima, in no less terror, ran along the other side of the iron grating to me, almost crying. Leaving him with Yura, I went to the station director, who, although cursing me, nevertheless gave the order to open the gate. Finally, we all got to the "room for mothers and children" and began to consider our further actions. Pyatigorsk, toward which we were going was still very far away and how would we get there? I remembered that my good friend Vera had formerly lived in Gorki. It was possible that she had never moved. I had not had any news from her since the beginning of the war. First, I had to find a telephone the very existence of which I was no longer sure. For almost six months the telephone was like something that had disappeared into eternity. I was happily surprised when not only a telephone but even a telephone book were at my disposal. I found Vera very easily. She was even still living in that very apartment in which she had lived 18 years ago. She invited us all to her place. Not hoping to find any kind of transportation at such a late hour, we set out on foot. From the station it was about five versts. Again a happy coincidence. An empty streetcar was standing in the square. It was making its last trip to the city center to which we wanted to go. We got out at Chernii Prud,* a place still known to me from childhood, where we used to go ice skating as children. The city had changed very much in the 17 years in which I had not lived in it and the complete blackout helped make it appear even more strange and foreign. There was a great deal of snow. Apparently here too as in other cities

* *Chernii Prud, or Black Pond, is a bus stop near a famous skating rink with the same name that is as familiar to people from Gorki as Times Square is to New Yorkers* [ED.].

there was no one to remove it. In the middle of the street there was a narrow path between the huge banks of snow. We moved in file. The whole picture gave a feeling of unreality. In addition to all this, fatigue and all the excitement that we had gone through were affecting us. It began to seem to me that I was asleep and dreaming. Sometimes in a dream you have the feeling that you have been here already, gone along this road, seen this place, the city, the house, but at the same time you cannot give yourself a clear account and remember when and where this was. You cannot find what you are striving for and you start wandering about without a goal. I uttered these thoughts aloud and frightened Yura. He began to cry. Finally, all the same, we got to the house where Vera lived with her daughter Natasha. This meant that fortunately we again had a roof over our heads.

APRIL 11

The very next day after our arrival Yura and I went to a doctor, who had formerly treated our whole family. It turns out that he is now a very important person, a member of the Lensoviet * and extremely influential in this city. His important position has not changed his character. He remains the same dear Uncle Sasha, as we used to call him. He received us surprisingly warmly and immediately gave us a few letters of recommendation to various important persons of highly responsible positions in the city. His

---

* *The Lensoviet were special councils whose members held a special status among the Soviet party workers, or "Apparatchiki." They are somewhat comparable to American city councils* [ED.].

name had a magic influence. We did not have to
stand for a long time in front of the door of the city
council. I gave the clerk checking my documents the
letter from Uncle Sasha. From force of habit I had
been prepared to wait for a long time. This clerk of
the city commission pushed aside the people standing
ahead of me and amiably invited us to follow him. He
led us straight to the office of the secretary of the
Gorki Party Committee, before whom the whole city
trembled. In ten minutes I had left with three documents in my hands; two were for special rations, and
one was for leaving Gorki by a special transport going in the direction of the Caucasus.

APRIL 13

The food we received thanks to the documents of the
city council brought complete delight and amazement to both Vera and Natasha. Hunger was also
reigning in Gorki. Food, which had been issued by
ration cards since the very first days of the war, was
very limited. It was often impossible even to receive
the minimum which was allotted to each inhabitant
of Gorki. Something or other was always lacking.
The food issued us at the two distribution points was
enough for several families. More important yet was
the fact that there were items included in these rations which the inhabitants of the city had not seen
since the beginning of the war.

APRIL 15

Today I undertook a number of steps in connection
with our departure. Since Pyatigorsk was listed as
the destination on our evacuation pass, the Gorki ad-

ministration, despite the recommendations of Uncle Sasha, will not be very happy with a prolonged stay on our part in Gorki. I cannot forget our stay in Cherepovets and the eternal begging for ration cards. Besides, the war is felt very strongly in Gorki. There are often interruptions even in the delivery of bread. People run from one shop to the other and return with empty hands. Of course, they are not starving as in Leningrad, since the countryside supplies milk and vegetables. However, the price of these products is beyond the reach of the average inhabitant: a liter of milk is 60 rubles, a kilo of carrots is also 60, butter is 700 rubles a kilo and so on. I have 4,000 rubles with me; this is less than enough for 6 kilos of butter.

The blackout constantly reminds one of the threatening danger. From time to time planes, apparently hostile, fly over, and the antiaircraft guns fire; somewhere or other bombs fall. One hears constant talk about the rapid advance of the Germans, about the taking of new cities and inhabited points. They even say that Gorki can be threatened by the German invasion. The latter I believe is simply the imagination of the "jittery." Nevertheless we better get to work on our departure. To survive Leningrad and then suffer in Gorki is not too wise.

APRIL 18

Although I fully understand the necessity of leaving, I am sorry to leave Gorki, a town where I spent my childhood and youth. Under the protection of Uncle Sasha we are living well. We can get as much food as we want. Everybody somehow or other acts very well toward us, and tries to help us in many ways. Out of curiosity I glanced into one of Uncle Sasha's letters which I had not yet handed in; I did this in order to understand the reason for our exceptional treatment from the "mighty rulers of the universe." Reading it through I laughed until the tears came. Uncle Sasha, well knowing the customs of our authorities, has promoted my husband to the administrator of the Leningrad military region, when he was in fact only the transport commander of one of the numerous evacuation points. Fortunately the Gorki administration either did not figure this out or did not want to figure it out, for this pass was signed by Doctor Ivanov, who carries so much weight in Gorki that it was impossible even to begin to doubt the accuracy of his words.

APRIL 20

Vera begs me not to leave Gorki and the local organization advises us to go to Siberia on a special transport going to Lake Baikal. Again I vacillate and do not know what to decide. Both proposals are tempting. Baikal is so far, that the war will never get there. Again my doubts are decided by other circumstances. I received a telephone call from the head of the Gorki evacuation center to whom I also had given a letter of recommendation from Uncle Sasha. He informed me that this very day a train of three cars would leave, headed south toward Mineralnye Vody, near Pyatigorsk. There would be room for all of us. We packed in a hurry. Except for the bread we had as emergency rations, we left our food with Vera. We even had the luxury of a taxi ride to the station, where the cars of the special transport to the Caucasus were already waiting. Here we found people like ourselves, evacuees from Leningrad who had been detained in Gorki. We took our places in the boxcars, which were conveniently arranged. A "second floor" was set up with wooden shelves, on which one could sleep. In the center was a stove for cooking. Since there were not more than twenty people in each car, we had more than enough room. At first glance these people seemed respectable, not at all like those with whom we had to travel from Leningrad to Cherepovets. Moreover, it was a lovely spring evening, with the sun just setting. While we waited for departure, Vera and I stood on the banks of the flooding Oka and recalled our younger days in Gorki. We felt particularly close. Vera was also from the Volga area, from Saratov. She had married a childhood friend of mine the same year I married, and they had moved to Nizhni Novgorod (Gorki). Her child was born almost the same time as mine. There was much that bound us together. Now we had to separate at a troubled, menacing time, and for how long we could not even guess.

APRIL 23

Our old nana wished to leave the train at her home station, Obrochnoye, where her relatives lived. After all she had suffered and endured, the trip to the unknown Caucasus seemed frightening to her. Indeed I myself was going there not even knowing whether my husband's sister who formerly lived in Pyatigorsk was still alive. I had never received an answer to my telegram with inquiries from Cherepovets. I could not accept the responsibility of persuading nana to accompany us and we parted, also not knowing whether we would ever see each other again.

The separation with nana was made more acute by our melancholy recollections. We were riding past my father's former estate. The large old park shining through the still bare trees, the columns of the white house, the entrance gates, the wide paths going to the entrance, all this flashed in front of my eyes like a dream, calling to mind innumerable pictures of the past, of childhood, which remains like a bright spot in the memory of every person.

APRIL 25

Life does not allow one to give himself over to reminiscences and to grief. Today the man in charge of our car brought very disquieting news. We had been headed toward Povorino-Stalingrad, but the railroad command had changed routes and turned our transport toward the station of Liske, from which the road went to Rostov. We began to discuss the new situation which had arisen and were disturbed by the lack of worry of the railroad men; this road passed not far from the front line and most important of all, along it there were no evacuation points which had been supplying us, the refugees, with food.

APRIL 27

We were taken to the Liske station and forgotten. We are on line 13. There is no one around. Some kind of half destroyed railroad cars are standing around. Everything is a frozen waste. Our situation is getting threatening. Our food supplies have not been replenished for several days. Even water is difficult to obtain. Fortunately for us we had received so much bread in Gorki that not only are we not hungry but we even shared some of ours with one woman with two children who had eaten all the bread she brought with her. However, if this situation will continue we will starve again. Dima is simply terror-stricken. More than anything else he fears a repetition of the Leningrad starvation. He believes that our car director is not energetic enough. He convinced the other occupants of our car to entrust their request for our departure to me. As a result they all did indeed decide that in such a situation it is easier for a woman to obtain something—and they elected me as the representative of our little transport. All the women and children went with me. En route, in order to encourage them, I reminded them that the 1917 revolution in Petrograd was started by women who were tired of standing in line for bread and had gone out into the streets with signs demanding "bread."

In our first effort at the city Soviet we had a complete fiasco. The director of the city Soviet, to whom we had all gotten through in a crowd, remained unshakable. Our delegation made no impression on him. In spite of all our entreaties he kept repeating the same thing, "I do not have any evacuation points. Who is supposed to give you bread? I cannot allot you any of the rations for the city population. Then they would all starve." Trying to use all my beautiful oratory I pointed out that from the year's supplies he could allot something to 20 persons so as to prevent the people, who had broken out of the blockade, from dying in the Liske station. Nothing helped. The government representative, who by the way looked in prime condition, remained firm and even began to get annoyed with our requests. The sight of suffering women and children did not touch him in the least. Looking at his dull, red face, I thought that he probably helped himself to the supplies entrusted to him, but of course, I did not dare say anything like that, fearing to spoil our position still further, and feeling also the responsibility for the entire car. Thus having obtained nothing, we left the first point of our hopes. Our next stop was the NKVD, where we managed to convince the guard who gave us some supper ration coupons. This was a great achievement. It is true that these coupons would not suffice for all of us, but we nonetheless did divide them so that everyone received something. Now we had to achieve the most important thing—the rapid dispatch of our three cars to the Caucasus. We had to convince the station manager of this. The railroad men turned out to be the most reasonable and receptive people. Besides it was clear to them that some kind of misunderstanding had occurred in connection with our train and that some one of the officers had sent our train off on a distant supply track, where it could remain for a long time if we did not see the authorities and try to do something about it. Expressing themselves very sharply about their colleague who had permitted such a mistake, they promised to send our car on toward Rostov. We returned with this happy news and indeed, in half an hour the cars began to move; our cars were attached to some type of train and we left the unhappy station of Liske.

APRIL 29

We are approaching Rostov. Spring is in full bloom. The door of our car is closed only at night. The weather is wonderful. Fields, meadows, and villages flash by. Everything is bathed in the spring sun. Somehow it becomes easier to live, and hopes for a better future again appear. Yura occupies a place in front of the wide open door from early morning until late in the evening. He is very curious and alert and everything interests him. Peasants have begun to appear at the stations exchanging various articles of food for clothing and other things. Money has lost all its value. Wherever the train stops, a whole market opens up immediately. The women of our car unpack their baggage and are happy to receive food in exchange. Eggs, milk, butter, and other fresh country products are more valuable than jewels. It is difficult to convey by words the happiness of the occupants of the car who are no longer menaced by starvation. Everything in life is so relative! Could I have even thought only one year ago that the possession of a two pound supply of butter and a few dozen eggs would fill me with such boundless happiness?

MAY 1

We have passed Rostov and are breathing quite freely. This is the route along which many have been evacuated; at every station there are special centers where bread and dinner is issued by cards. The main thing now is the wonderful spring weather; all around us is a plush sea of white blossoms of apple and other fruit trees. It is warm as in the summer and we are dressed for winter. We have just passed Armavir, where on the occasion of the First of May we received a magnificent dinner: soup, cutlets with potatoes, and compote for dessert.

MAY 2

We are approaching Mineralnye Vody. Gavrilova, who made the whole journey with us from Cherepovets, and keeps me from sleeping at times with her fears that they were sending us by such a dangerous route—close to the front line, now is again agitated and does not sleep at night, sighing without stop. She cannot decide whether to continue her trip with us or go to Baku to her husband's relatives. I do not try to persuade her one way or the other. In the first place I myself am going into the complete unknown, and in the second place, as we say, "in misfortune people reveal themselves." Indeed, it is in misfortune that we have gotten to know her well. Let her arrange her further fate by herself or with the aid of relatives! Fortunately she decided to go to Baku. Now it is three o'clock in the afternoon. In an hour we will be in Mineralnye Vody and then transfer to Pyatigorsk. What is awaiting us there?

Pyatigorsk

May 3 to August 9, 1942

We warmly took leave with all the passengers of our car, with whom we had lived so closely for these two weeks of travel. We detrained on the platform for Mineralnye Vody. Soon the train was going to Kislovodsk approached us. Somehow, with the aid of other persons on the platform who guessed that we were Leningrad evacuees—it turns out that more than one train from Leningrad had already come to the Caucasus—we got into a train which seemed to us like a wonderful, fairy-tale train after the ones we traveled in since our evacuation from Leningrad. Everything seemed as unbelievable as in a dream. The passengers around us were in summer clothes and were happy and cordial. The cars shone with cleanliness; beyond the windows flashed the charming glimpses of the foothills of the Caucasus. At the beginning of May the grass was still fresh, green, and the flowers created an impression of a rich, colorful carpet. We, in our winter coats and the boys in their military helmets that had been given to them in the hospital train by their friends, presented a rather strange picture on this spring evening. The southerners are an open, expansive people and noisily express their sympathy and feelings. Questioning us about our experiences, the war, the blockade, and the famine, they oh and ah and give advice. Gradually my fear of the unknown gives way to a feeling of assurance that even if we do not find my husband's sister, we shall not be lost among these people.

In Pyatigorsk the whole car helped us get out and unload our things and showered us with all kinds of good wishes. The train left. We stood on the platform and searched with our eyes for somebody who could take us to the address I had. It was hot. The sun was baking unbearably. To take off all our warm clothing and carry it seemed still more difficult. Finally a helpful person sent us a man with a wheelbarrow on which we placed all our things. We put our furs and coats on top and set out on a new expedition. The entire city is in bloom. One's head spins from the pungent, stupefying odor. For the first time in the entire ten months of the war I felt so exhausted that I was afraid of losing consciousness. I moved along in a semidelirium holding on to the handle of the barrow and in front of my eyes some kind of black butterflies seemed to be flying and kept me from seeing the road. The boys were walking along cheerfully, enjoying the spring weather, the sun, and the wonderful nature. The main thing is that we have reached the goal of our journey. I did not share with them my doubts about the possibility of Lyalya's not being there. I consoled myself with the thought that if we did not find anyone, we would settle on the street and wait for what comes. As the proverb says, "The world is not without good people." We went to the house—Kochura Street 34. Not a soul was at the windows. The entrance is through a garden. And here everything is in full bloom and fragrant. We turned the corner and approached the porch. Sitting on the steps and tanning in the sun was a familiar figure, my husband's niece Tanya, whom we had last seen in Leningrad six months ago.

MAY 5

My husband's mother, sister, and children received us with heart-felt joy and set us up in their apartment, despite the fact that they were living under very crowded conditions—7 persons in 3 rooms. With us it made 10. Lyalya did not want to hear about us seeking another apartment and, to tell the truth, it would have been impossible for us to get anything. It had always been very difficult to get an apartment and now with the mass of evacuees from Leningrad and other places threatened by the war, the housing situation had become very bad. We found out that all institutions of higher education from Leningrad had been sent to Pyatigorsk: the Mining Institute, the Pedagogical, the Economics, etc. This means that the Caucasus is not considered a danger zone from the military point of view. This is calming news to us.

The main event of yesterday was our trip to the market. Yura was completely ecstatic about such a quantity of food, mountains of butter, lard, apples, nuts, and vegetables. It was a genuine market as in peacetime. But the prices are not "peacetime" ones. Nevertheless, in comparison with Gorki they are much lower. Butter can be bought for 150 rubles a kilo, milk for 10–12 rubles a liter and meat for 70 rubles a kilo. I bought everything that caught the ecstatic gaze of Yura. Dima, being older and knowing my limited means, held himself back but he could not take his eyes off such a wealth of food, the likes

of which he has not seen for so long. At the market
we ran into the actors of the Radlovski theatre,
among whom was our old friend Bolkhovskoi whom
we had not seen since before the war. The theatre
had been evacuated from Leningrad several months
ago and the actors enthusiastically told me about the
wonderful life in Pyatigorsk.

JUNE 8

The medical commission pronounced me a temporary
invalid. The Leningrad famine had weakened me and
I am not capable of working. I shall receive a pension
of 200 rubles a month. In addition to that I am receiving 500 rubles for the military certificate of my
husband. Lyalya earns 800 rubles a month in the
sewing workshop. This is considered an outstanding
salary by local standards. But, of course, it is impossible to live on that salary. Her husband's pay is 300
rubles and her daughter Verochka is still in school.
Her son Kolya and his wife have fled here from Kiev
which has been occupied by the Germans. Her niece
Tanya has come here from Leningrad. They are very
strained financially. The old grandmother is manag-
ing the household, receiving 30 rubles daily for ex-
penses from her daughter. For this money it is possible to buy shavel (a green, cereal grass used for
soup) and potatoes. By cooking these items for hours
over a kerosene burner, soup is obtained. This is the
only dish for supper. They do not have the money to
buy other foods at the market at the black market
prices. I can see that here too things will not be easy.
Yesterday I managed to get passes to the Leningrad
cafeteria, located in the railroad station building.
There they feed well. For us, Leningraders, in addi-

tion to the cafeteria there is still one store. This store the local inhabitants regard with that same envy which we once had for the Leningrad Torgsin Exchange, where it was possible to buy virtually anything—but only for foreign currency, or gold or silver. At this store we received an excellent ration, including even sugar, which the local inhabitants have not seen for a long time. Grandmother's delight was indescribable when I gave her half. For the children I received candy as well. Leningraders are a special category.

JUNE 9

Nonetheless, since my finances cannot really sustain us for long, I am thinking about work. I went to one establishment where they are looking for a typist. It turned out that they pay 350 rubles a month, in other words, a little more than two kilos of butter. My work would take all my time and then I would have to give up the pension. In addition I would have to convince the medical commission that I am capable of work. And even then the total difference is only 150 rubles. As they say "it is just not worth it." Noticing that one entire corner of Lyalya's room was piled high with some type of cloth scraps, I asked her about it. She said that she is allowed to take home from the shop all remnants if they are under a certain size. During the period she has been working there she has accumulated an entire pile of scraps which is not being used for anything and only gives the room a disorderly appearance. The idea suddenly came to me of sewing these pieces into children's clothes and aprons and selling them at the market. For a long time it has been impossible to buy any

kind of manufactured items in the Pyatigorsk stores.
The sewing shop in which Lyalya is working belongs
to the NKVD and the wives of the NKVD members
can shop in special stores. At first my idea seemed
fantastic to everyone, but we decided to try it just
the same. All the young ones set to work. Tanya sews
better than anyone else. In addition she has good
taste. Zina, Kolya's wife, and Vera, his sister, help.
I am a terrible seamstress but under Tanya's direction I too create something. I hope that my "works of
art" will attract somebody too.

JUNE 10

Unbelievable success! Dima and our happy, energetic
neighbor Dina, sold all our products in less than two
hours. What I had not known earlier was that even
before the war it was very difficult to get material in
Pyatigorsk and there was a great shortage of goods
and clothes. From time to time these items would be
brought from the great urban centers but they would
be sold out right away. With the coming of the war
everything disappeared. Thus, Dima proudly brought
us a sum equal to more than half of Lyalya's monthly
salary.

JUNE 15

Our work is bustling along at full speed. When
Lyalya saw that the mountain of rags gradually was
being transformed into thousands of rubles, she too
became happy. During the two weeks that we have
been here, we had even forgotten to think about the
war, since we were occupied with all the material
worries about getting established here. On the radio

no disquieting news is transmitted. Some places are taken, others retaken. The impression is that everything is being stabilized. Maybe the war will end soon?

JUNE 16

Knowing that our Leningrad Pedagogical Institute where I had studied had also been transferred to Pyatigorsk, I went today to the office and there I found out the welcome news that teachers will be needed starting in autumn. I am on the list and can count on working in my specialty from the first of September. The young ones are being sent out to do field work; however, the doctors rejected Dima for work since he still has not recovered from the consequences of dystrophy.

JUNE 20

I finally have begun to receive letters from relatives— and it is a constant lament! My aunt, who lived in our apartment in Leningrad and who was evacuated to Siberia along with Ludmilla and her children, writes that she exchanged a large part of her belongings for food and that life is still very difficult. My cousin is working in the railroad canteen, but her salary just suffices to feed herself. My aunt and the children can only exist by exchanging their possessions. But how much could they have taken with them from Leningrad? My cousin Vasya, the actor, who earned a lot of money and was a great success prior to the war, now is receiving so little that he had to sell his gold watch. However, the markets in Siberia are loaded with excellent goods since there are a great number

of evacuees from all the big cities and they exist
mainly by bartering their belongings. My cousin,
Marina, whom I had intended to visit when I was
working on the hospital train, was able to evacuate to
Perm. She writes from the Perm vicinity that they
were fed poorly even at first, but now it has gotten
much worse. The rations have reached an absolute
minimum and she begs me to help her get established
in Pyatigorsk.

JUNE 25

Finally I am in correspondence with my husband. He
had lost track of us completely. At the end of March
he was able to get an assignment to Tikhvin where
Dima had been at the beginning of March. There he
accidentally found out about Dima's stay there from
one of his co-workers. However, he was too late to
get hold of Dima who had already been evacuated.
My husband then began to search for him in all the
hospitals but could get no exact information except
that Dima had been evacuated. One of my letters
nevertheless did get through to my husband and he
went to Cherepovets in the hope of finding us there.
However, in Cherepovets he found out that we had
left, but nobody could tell him for where. My landlords assured him that we had gone to Siberia to our
cousin and at the evacuation center they assured him
that we must be on the road to the Caucasus. He began to write to all addresses, but for over two
months, he was completely in the dark as to our
whereabouts. The postal service in the frontal zone
was functioning poorly and none of my letters
reached him. Finally he received a telegram from
my aunt in Siberia who informed him that I was

working in a hospital car and that the children were with me. He was relieved. But nevertheless further contact was again lost. Mail to and from Siberia went better and I was constantly writing to our aunt. She, having found out that we had reached the Caucasus safe, and sound, informed my husband about this. And so yesterday I received a long letter from him with a description of his trials and tribulations in searching for us. He wrote that his spirits have definitely lifted since he knows that we are out of danger and that now it will be easier for him to endure all the physical deprivations connected with the blockade. From his letter one can see that the situation in Leningrad is still very tense: frequent shellings and bombardments. The food situation is also very difficult; people had become so weak during the terrible winter that all the insignificant supplements of bread helped little, and as before there are no other foods. He has set up a little garden in the garage and there he has planted radishes, carrots, and other vegetables. It is to be hoped that this lot will support him in the course of the summer. Among other things he writes that shavel, a cereal grass, has appeared on the market at 1000 rubles a kilogram (5 rubles in Pyatigorsk) and those who have such money are buying it, happy to eat such essential vitamins, instead of oil cakes and paste. He supplied me with news about friends and acquaintances. Some had succeeded in evacuating; others, for example, my friend Irina Levitskaya, are lying in a hospital thanks to the efforts of my husband. The hospital is the salvation for everyone. There they feed better and regularly several times a day. To be hospitalized is very difficult. One has to have connections. Everybody has the same need to get into the hospital. My husband writes that since spring, the mortality rate among women has increased greatly. Until now somehow or other they had held out better.

JUNE 28

I received another letter from Leningrad—from the wife of the technical director of the kombinat, where my husband had worked until the war. She writes that the Leningraders ate up all the grass and even the leaves from the trees and that the population has noticeably diminished. While many had been evacuated in the spring by ship, most of the loss was due to death from hunger. Altogether death had taken more than half.

Life in Pyatigorsk is carried on completely by "blat." * Everything can be obtained by "acquaintance." Bribery and corruption in all forms are flourishing. This is especially evident among the evacuees. The Leningraders have lived so long under the fear of death by starvation that they are especially afraid of a possible repetition of this fate. The amount of the rations issued is being diminished. And although at first, these "generous" rations might seem grandiose to people on the very brink of starvation, they consist in fact of only some 800 grams of sugar a month, 400 grams of candy, some fats, and so on. Of course these cannot suffice for a month under any conditions. There is some talk about the closing of the dining hall. The supply of rations is not sufficient to feed the increasing number of evacuees not only from Leningrad but also from other cities. A few days ago something occurred which made me extremely

* *Political pull or connections* [ED.].

happy. Every day I buy my bread in a certain shop where there is a young, very beautiful clerk. She had not previously shown any great friendliness nor had we had anything to talk about. The third day by accident I came a little early and the bread had not been delivered yet. There was no one around and we began to talk. As if in passing she mentioned to me, "You have fine perfume, bring me some and I will give you white bread." * White bread was such a rarity that it was issued only by special tickets to highly placed individuals. Fearing "provocation" I did not bring it. The next day, seizing an occasion, the girl again asked me. So today I poured out some perfume and took it to the shop. I received a double portion of bread. Everywhere it is the same.

JUNE 30

I am continuing to receive a double portion of bread and I have no qualms of conscience. Perhaps the salesgirl cut the rations of some one of these "mighty rulers of the universe" who are so well supplied that they are not paying attention as to whether we have enough now for our whole family. Lyalya, who is working in the NKVD dressmaking shop, also receives various gifts from her customers. From some of these gifts you can get an idea of how well they live. Once she brought a huge piece of pork. Everybody was overjoyed by such a large amount of meat. But Lyalya's stepdaughter, who was present at the

---

* *How ironical! In Leningrad because of different conditions of living, gold or precious items such as jewelry, rare materials, fine leathergoods and so on were only exchangeable against food. Here in a small provincial city, even a little perfume had some trading value* [AUTHOR].

time, convinced Lyalya to marinate this "treasure" according to one of her special recipes. Lyalya, who was under her strong influence, agreed. But after several days when they opened the dish with the marinated pork, they found it infested with worms. The anger of Lyalya's children and her mother was unlimited. The whole problem consisted in hiding this situation from the hungry neighbors. At night it was necessary to dig a deep grave in the corner of the garden to bury the remains of the pork.

The population of Pyatigorsk is also starving. The only thing that saves them is the small garden plots where they have planted different types of vegetables. Some have relatives living in the country, who supply them with fruits and dairy products, but these are the exceptions. The prices on the market are so high that they are completely inaccessible to the inhabitants. The rations authorized by cards are so minimal that it is not even worth talking about.

Today, while passing the market, I again met Bolkhovskoi. In Leningrad we were not such close acquaintances, but now we greet each other like old friends. All that we have suffered has somehow drawn all the Leningraders together in a special way. Thus the very word "Leningrader" has a special meaning for us. Bolkhovskoi invited us to see his performance in the summer theatre, in the flower garden, where he will give an artistic reading of *Anna Karenina*. We decided to go with Tanya and Dima. It seems a little strange that it is still possible to lead a normal life, even to go to the theater, to meet people with whom it is possible to speak not only about our "daily bread."

JULY 3

There is a lot we do not find out from the newspapers. But rumors are circulating from all directions that the Germans have again begun to advance. On the radio they transmit accounts about the unbelievable bestiality perpetrated by the Germans in the territories they have occupied. When you hear all this your heart again begins to feel heavy, as it did a year ago in Leningrad. Is it really possible that the enemy will reach the Caucasus and that we will again be in the trap. I am beginning to regret strongly that I did not go with the children to Siberia from Gorki, while it was still possible. Life, however, runs its course. We forget about the rumors and enjoy the wonderful summer weather and the beauties of Pyatigorsk and its surroundings. Everywhere we meet Leningraders. In the cafeteria, in the store; with many we became acquainted; with a number of others we developed friendships. I also met old acquaintances, teachers, and students from our Institute. We are leading an almost normal, prewar life. We go to the movies, to the theatre. I rode with Tanya to Essentuki to a "famous" fortune-teller. This woman, together with her husband and son, was evacuated from Kharkov at the very beginning of the war. En route they came under fire. Her husband was killed by a shell and although she lost both legs, she survived. Her son was called into the army from Essentuki and she was left to the care of sympathetic neighbors. She took up fortune-telling. She has a huge clientele. In these anxious times everyone hopes for some type of miracle. The city authorities do not persecute her for this type of enterprise. Apparently they look the other way. This

visit left me with a very morose impression. There is
no limit to human sorrow. In comparison to her it
seems that what we have been through is not so terrible as it had seemed. From all that she told me, one
thing stood out: in the near future we will again have
to undertake a long journey and we must not hesitate,
we must leave. And in the more distant future she
foresaw some type of travel not only on land but on
water. Is it possible that we will have to wander our
whole life? It is of course stupid to believe in all these
predictions, but I can already see us, fleeing from the
advancing army across the Caspian Sea into the
steppes of Kazakhstan. Tanya is more interested in
the fate of her little daughter, whom she had left in
Leningrad and whom Tanya's mother had promised
to bring to Pyatigorsk with the next transport. When
Tanya left Leningrad there was a terrible frost and
her mother convinced her to leave her daughter for
the meantime, being sure that they would be able to
evacuate a few days later. But it did not turn out that
way. A thaw had followed the frosts and the road
across Ladoga was closed. When communication was
again opened by water, new difficulties arose. As a result Tanya was separated from her mother and her
four-year-old daughter.

JULY 10

Young people are being recruited at an increased rate
for the digging of trenches. This is a bad sign. Today
Milochka, our neighbor's daughter, was sent there
from the school where she studies. Her mother is upset. Not long ago her husband died in the war and
now she has so much worry about her daughter.
There is no one to help her with Victor, her son. This

boy is an impossible hooligan and now he is left on his own, since his mother goes off to work in the hospital at eight in the morning and returns at five. Victor spends the whole day in the streets and gets Yuri into all kinds of things he thinks up. Sometimes they take off for somewhere or other and it is impossible to find them. For me too this is an endless source of worry. All is not well in Lyalya's family either. Her youngest son, the eighteen-year-old Mitya, has been called to the army and there has been no news from him for several months. Lyalya's daughter Olga recently married a young lieutenant, with whom she had become acquainted while working at the hospital where he was lying wounded. At present the lieutenant is on leave at his parents and she is with him. However, he will soon be sent again to the front. Lyalya's oldest son, Kolya, is a semiinvalid; he had paralysis as a child and he was exempted from military service. Now he is working in Pyatigorsk, but for the very minimum wage. And with this he has to support his wife Zina. Their first child died in the winter, a winter which was very difficult for the people of Pyatigorsk. There was a shortage of fuel for there are no woods in the vicinity, and there was a great shortage of food. Zina's milk dried up. Artificial feeding of children is still in its rudimentary stages and the situation is made worse since there are interruptions in the delivery of milk. The youngest, Verochka, is still studying in school. Lyalya herself married a third time to a certain Krasinski. Her second husband, Androvich, a Jew, from whom she had three children, died a few years ago. He was traveling on an official assignment and was carrying a portfolio containing important papers and money. Some criminals pushed him from the train which was going at full speed and his head was cut off. When Lyalya now hears of the crimes committed by the Germans toward the Jewish population she trembles in fear for the fate of her daughters and Mitya. Many Jews have already left the Caucasus and are moving deep into the country. Lyalya does not have either the money or the transportation; nor does she have the necessary energy for such a move. Krasinski does not give any help whatsoever. He makes the most negative impression on us all. Lyalya's mother simply hates him and calls him Vanka-Klyuchnik (the key man). He always has keys; even when he sleeps he keeps them under his pillow. During the day he carries them on his belt and very deliberately locks everything, afraid that someone's going to steal something. We all wonder about him and ask ourselves the question just what, to tell the truth, is he locking. There are no valuables or money in the house. Also, the children and friends had become accustomed to the generosity of the deceased Ilya Androvich. The latter was so generous that everything he had was at the disposal of anyone who wanted it. Now things are changed. Lyalya does not allow herself to contradict Krasinski; the children grumble but do not protest openly. This is so obnoxious to me that I am thinking about moving to another apartment. Moreover, we are badly crowded; Dima, Yura, and I have quartered ourselves behind a screen in the dining room. If anyone of the neighbors comes over we cannot lie down to sleep, but have to wait until everyone leaves. It is very uncomfortable. We do not have our own nook. Then on top of this there is Ivan who wakes us up in the morning, rattling his keys and checking the contents of the wardrobe which is behind the screen in our corner. I mentioned our plans about moving to

Lyalya but she begged me to stay. I do not want to hurt her but it is impossible to even think about having peace and quiet.

JULY 12

Youth forgets more quickly than do others about the war and the impending danger of the Germans seizing the Caucasus. They give themselves up to all types of amusements. A few days ago I met one of my Leningrad acquaintances, an engineer Pospelov, and invited him to visit us. He apparently is captivated by Tanya, a pretty blue-eyed blonde, and now he spends every evening at our place. He offered his help to Zina, Tanya, and Vera who were watering the garden. They could think of nothing better than to sprinkle him with water from head to foot. I thought that he would not forgive this, but today he again appeared as if nothing had taken place. Olga, Lyalya's eldest daughter from her second marriage, also came. Olga's husband Nickolai is being transferred to another military unit and she is going to accompany him. Then she will stay in the East since her husband feels that there is danger to the Caucasus. The Germans are trying to get possession of our oil. Baku is already too tempting a morsel for Hitler.

JULY 15

I went to Kislovodsk to look for my friend from Leningrad, Rimma Gordon. It turned out that she and her husband and daughter had succeeded in evacuating the Caucasus last year, soon after their arrival from Leningrad. Indeed last summer the Germans were advancing rapidly along the entire length of the front. Since the Gordons are Jewish, I believe that they acted wisely. On the radio there are constant announcements of what is happening in the occupied districts. One's common sense does not accept it but you must not disbelieve everything. Olga is very insistent that her mother take Vera and leave for the East.

JULY 20

I am receiving letters regularly from my husband. He writes that now he is enduring all the trials of the blockade with equanimity, for he knows that we are in complete security. Apparently, these have just been idle rumors about the Germans seizing the Caucasus. Much panic is being created all around. My husband begs us to send him some photos; he cannot believe that we have again acquired a human appearance. The main subject in his letters is still his fear of hunger. He is afraid that we might experience food shortages even here in the Caucasus. He does not really believe my assurance that everything is all right in this respect. Of course his mood is completely comprehensible to me. For we were indifferent to everything, including bombs and the shelling, when we felt that we eventually would die from hunger. Hunger cannot be compared with any other kind of misfortune. I remember how I went to the cafeteria with my friend Zhenya under vicious shelling and running from one house to another, from one gateway to another, not even dreaming about returning without having received dinner. And still another instance: with that very same Zhenya, I had gone to the Mikhailovski Castle where a hospital had been set up, to look up some close friends, a husband and wife, who were working as doctors in this hospital. They, of course, received a rather decent ration for their work. At that time the Mikhailovski Castle was the very incarnation of that dark idea which we all connect with it. In the Mikhailovski Castle on the night of March 11, 1801, Tsar Paul had been strangled. Even in the brightest days of my life in Leningrad this castle gave me the impression of being connected with the history of this cruel murder. Now, however, going inside and asking the names of our friends we were forced to pass a series of dark rooms lighted only by small wick lamps, since the electricity was not functioning any longer. Everywhere, even in the corridors, there were wounded lying about, looking more like ghosts and apparitions than like living people. From everywhere the echoing of moans and groans could be heard. We were happy when we got to the narrow back stairway which led to the doctor's apartment. But right there began the real trial. The entire stairway was covered with ice and the steps were not visible. This was simply an ice mountain. At this time the water pipes burst and repairing them was out of the question. We began to crawl, afraid of losing our balance and hurtling down. Such an ascent could only be dreamt about in a nightmare, but we stubbornly kept on going up, driven by one hope, that our friends would share their own more abundant rations with us. But complete disappointment awaited us there when we arrived. Although our avid eyes immediately noted that there was not only bread but even black caviar on the table, they immediately gave us to understand that we could not count on their help. To such a degree had hunger made people cruel.

131

JULY 24

Today is my name day. Lyalya had received white flour and butter for sewing a fine dress for the wife of the NKVD commander. I took some sugar out of the rations that we, as evacuated Leningraders, had received, and a tea like in peacetime was arranged. Pirogi and vatrushki with cherries and apricots from our garden were prepared tastefully, and we celebrated this day, even inviting our neighbors, the Bekovis, as guests. Since our family had by this time grown to twelve persons, this made twenty persons in all. Tomorrow Olga and her husband are leaving. They are stubbornly trying to persuade Lyalya to abandon everything and go with them across the Caspian Sea to a secure area. Nikolai suggests that we must all make this decision and not hesitate a minute. But how can we make this trip? We have almost no money. Nobody will give us transportation; it is virtually impossible to rent horses even at fantastic prices. Those four thousand rubles, my iron reserve, have long since gone. My "invalid" pension and the military allotment of my husband will be all that we will receive. But even these revenues are like crumbs when compared with the fantastically rising prices in the country.

Kolya, Lyalya's son from her first marriage, is less pessimistic. He does not even admit the possibility that the Germans will reach the Caucasus. In that case, according to him, the war would be over. If Baku falls we would be deprived of our oil and the Volga route would be cut. Besides that, he does not see any genuine possibility of our moving beyond the Caspian Sea, considering the age and illness of our grandmother, whom we could not leave, and taking into consideration our complete lack of money or means of movement.

JULY 27

Today Lyalya was offered transportation for three. What a riddle. Whom to take, whom to leave? Of course there could be no thought of taking us or Tanya. But it was even impossible to take the closest members of the family. Grandmother categorically announced that she would remain in any case. Ivan is trembling like an autumn leaf both from the fear of the trip and from the fear of being left. His egotism and his cowardice are both revealed. Lyalya does not know what to decide and an answer is demanded right away. Remembering how I suffered because of my indecisiveness I advised her to go. The main thing was to take Verochka away and the third one to go would have to be Ivan. She should not forget that Verochka was half Jewish which meant that she was severely threatened. We, that is, I, my children, Tanya, Kolya, Zina, and grandmother would remain in the meantime and we would look for some other possibility of evacuation, either through the military commissariat, from where I receive my allowance for my husband, or through the place where Kolya works. There they have hinted to him about the possibility of evacuation.

JULY 30

Today Lyalya was refused transportation. It turns out that there is not even space for the most responsible workers. I went to the Military Commissariat to find out what possibilities there were. I took all my documents and my husband's money voucher. A crowd of women was standing in front of the Commissariat; for the most part these were women with little children in their arms. They were waiting for a transportation authorization. I joined them. From the conversations it became clear that the majority of them were persons evacuated from Leningrad in the course of last winter. We waited for about two hours, but even then we did not see the transportation commander. A Red Army man came out and announced that the commander had been summoned somewhere on urgent business and today he would not see anyone. He advised us all to come back tomorrow. We left with heavy hearts; something extremely ominous is again moving toward us. Many women were crying and complaining that they had come out of the frying pan into the fire. They remembered Leningrad which now seemed to them somehow to be their own place, their home at least, even though it had been difficult there. But here they all felt foreign and lonely.

AUGUST 1

There is some kind of dark uneasiness in the city. Although the radio does not announce any especially threatening news, various information is still being transmitted about the new directions of the advance of the German army. Although all this is still far from us, things are not quite right. Lyalya's good friend, the manager of the canning kombinat, stopped in yesterday and offered us some canned goods. It seems rather strange that he is freely offering the use of canned goods which are the iron reserve of the city's food. Tanya and I ran there at the agreed time, very early in the morning, and were amazed at his generosity. He gave us so many cans that we could hardly drag them home. To our question whether he would drop in again in the next couple of days, he evasively answered that he was very busy. We were surprised. Formerly he had dropped in on us rather often, not bothering to think about his work.

Having finally obtained an audience with the Military Commissariat, I was turned down because of the absence of free transport. Today I met two women students from my Institute and they and a teacher told me that they were getting ready to leave on foot.

AUGUST 2

Today Yura and I rushed to the Military Commissariat to receive our money for my husband's voucher. While still in line we heard that there was no cashier and that we might as well forget about the money. The women left in great agitation, discussing what to do. Yura and I nonetheless managed to get inside the building. Without knocking, I rushed up to the cashier, who was getting ready to leave. I did receive my 500 rubles. But what could I do now with them? Rumors are reaching us that those waiting to be ferried across the Caspian had to pay 20 rubles just for a bucket of fresh water and for the crossing, thousands.

On the way home we noticed huge lines around the stores. Everywhere stores of food products which had not been seen by the population for a long time were being released for purchase. Sugar, butter, soap, and canned goods have appeared as if from out of the ground. We too succeeded in buying something. Whether we get out, or whether we are stuck here we will have to eat nonetheless. This to me was the most rational use of our wealth of 500 rubles. The prices on these foods were those fixed by the state firm. We returned home and faced a new problem. An order had been issued that all men from 16 to 55 should leave the city in units, on foot of course. Twenty-four hours after the issuing of this order anybody found on the street would be shot. It is difficult to convey in words the panic which engulfed our house and that of our neighbors.

AUGUST 3

Kolya is 24 years old and Ivan is 50. They both come under this order. In the evening, with a group of other men, not called to the army, in other words, invalids, they set out toward Nalchik, but nothing came out of this march. During the first few hours many took off to neighboring places and hid. Ivan and Kolya, dead tired and hungry, returned toward morning, deciding that it did not matter where they died.

Frightened by all these events, Lyalya rushed to the hospital to a doctor she knew with a request to assign her son and husband there temporarily. The hospital was overcrowded, but nonetheless the doctor put both of them in the corridor. Kolya had again developed rheumatism and had almost completely lost the use of one hand. They took Ivan to keep him company.

AUGUST 6

The evacuation is going on at an increasing speed but almost the only ones leaving are the "higher-ups." I have to compare this with the evacuation from Leningrad, where, in spite of all the disorder which reigned, there was nonetheless more justice. In Pyati-gorsk, however, a disgrace is taking place, a disgrace which is without limits. With my own eyes I saw how a family not only got themselves into a truck but took all their furniture and even firewood. It was difficult to believe my own eyes. But this is a sad fact—and it is not the only one.

On the corner of one of the streets nearest us a group of Jewish poor people were gathered. They had been crowding on this corner for two days, beg-ging the passing cars to take them. No one pays any attention. They cry, so that there is a constant, unin-terrupted howl. Today, while I was watching, they succeeded in stopping one Red Army truck. The sol-diers felt sorry and took several persons.

During the last few days the entire administration has disappeared. I went to the Institute—no one there. I asked where is the director? "Not here." The Dean? "Also not here." Where are they then? A teacher I knew called me aside and said, "Better not ask, they have fled, taking all the Institute money and stamps." When I went through the corridors, I met a group of professors, discussing the situation. The women were crying. All I hear is, "Was it worthwhile to ship us out of Leningrad in order to throw us here?" Two Jewish girls I knew as students in Leningrad met me. They were supposed to have left a few days ago with my French teacher. They rushed toward me in tears. I asked why they did not leave earlier. It seems that someone promised them all transport and had taken off. Still another teacher came up. She had a pack on her back and supplies of food for several days. She had decided to go on foot. I introduced her to the girls. She proposed that they join her. For the three of them the trip would not seem so fearful. From the

Institute we went along the street where the Military
Commissariat was located. Everything was locked.
There was a group of women on the street. From
their tears and wails you feel like crying. Not one of
the women had received money. The administration
had taken off. They had promised transport and evacuation, but that was just talk; they had not meant it.
Yesterday, however, at the last minute, they had suggested going by foot to Makhas-Kala; but almost all
these women have little children. Could they get far
with them? All I hear is, "Why did they ship us out of
Leningrad? It would at least have been better to die
at home." I ran to the insurance office where I received my invalid pension. A guard met me there
looking at me as though I had come from the moon.
"You want to get money? Money? The manager left
two days ago . . . his tracks have grown cold. He
took everything with him. Indeed you cannot get to
Kazakhstan for less than a thousand. He'll make use
of your money." The old guard still had his sense of
humor.

AUGUST 7

These are no longer rumors, but fact. The Germans
are near. The administration had evacuated in good
time taking the entire city transport, equipment,
money, wood, etc. The population, however, has been
abandoned to its fate. All our attempts to evacuate
either the entire family or individually met with no
success. We made arrangements with one family to
leave on horses but this plan did not work out either.
During the night someone took away the horses
which had already been prepared. The fear is so
great that no one bothers with anything. Today I

stood on that street where the military hospital had been established and observed how the wounded soldiers were hobbling on foot, leaving the city. And there was not even transportation for them! They went in single file, without arms, on crutches, with bandaged heads. The day is unbearably hot. The sun is baking.

AUGUST 8

Today our neighbor returned on foot from Nalchik, giving us news that made me feel good. The wounded blocked the road to commandeer a truck which was loaded with people, baggage, and fuel. They tossed out everyone and everything and took over the truck. The driver did not object and took them farther. At the present moment unrestrained pillaging of the city is taking place. There is no authority. Through the streets barrels of cooking oil, sacks of flour, whole sides of meat are being dragged. There is so much shouting and pushing in the streets! The people have been turned into animals. Our neighbors who were also going after this oil told us that there was such a fight around these barrels that people were actually pushed into them. It is frightening. How will all this looting end?

Rumors are circulating everywhere that tomorrow, the ninth, the city will be bombed. It is said that Rostov has already been taken, however, this has not been announced by the radio yet. A Red Army unit has set itself up on our street, Kochura. Trucks are standing there. The Red soldiers are sleeping on the ground. They are burnt black from the sun and are exhausted. Some are sitting morosely, dejectedly staring straight ahead, even their voices are not audible.

We ran into the garden, gathered the plums, peaches, and apples, and sent Yura, as the smallest of us, to take them to the soldiers. The latter accepted them with thanks, but did not enter into any kind of conversation with anybody. Some women, the wives of Red soldiers, went up to these men and asked them to take them with them. The commander came and ordered the women to disperse. Soon all the soldiers got on the trucks and rode away in the direction of Goryachevodsk.

AUGUST 8, *evening*

On the streets individual vehicles whiz past. In one of the cars on the main street we noticed one of the women with children who had been standing near us. Apparently she was lucky and had succeeded in persuading one of the soldiers to take her away. The other women looked at her with envy. A group of Red soldiers ran through our garden, jumping over the fence, throwing away some of their heavy things. It is said that they were seen near the power plant. Is it possible that they are going to blow it up?

We constantly feel drawn toward the street. It is impossible to sit still when there is such confusion everywhere. The main thing is that we want to find out from somebody what is really going on. It looks like a genuine rout of our army. Behind the fence of our garden we found a discarded rifle. It looks like panic.

AUGUST 9

I awoke at seven o'clock. A complete silence. It is as though last evening trucks had not been pounding over the pavement, as though alarm signals had not been sounding, as though the heavy Red Army boots had not tramped past our windows. And now it seems like a dream. Our charming little garden with its numerous fruit trees is drowned in the gleam of the sun's rays. There is not one cloud in the sky. I sat down on the front porch and did not want to leave as it was so pleasant on this wonderful August morning. Lyalya came to me. She was not going to work any longer. There was not anyone to sew for now. Her clientele had long since departed. Thanks to this silence and peace, one did not want to think about the war and about the German attack. Lyalya, however, insisted that I go with her to cover the little trench in front of the house with boards. This was something which we had long thought of doing but which we had always put off, not wishing to believe in danger. We went, dragging the old gates over there and covered them with earth.

The city was beginning to wake up. The housewives were dragging themselves to market. A group of neighbors went past us happily announcing that railroad cars loaded with flour were standing at the station.

Tanya, Yurochka, and I went toward the market deciding to spend our remaining money to buy some type, any type, of food. There was great animation at the market. Many people had gathered, selling, exchanging. We had just started to purchase our food when a deafening salvo resounded and the entire crowd scattered. We too ran from the marketplace to the city center. After this first salvo nothing followed. The population quickly calmed down, the supposition being expressed that it was possibly the explosion of the power plant which no one was guarding any longer. At this moment another, an extremely loud, artillery shot was heard, then another, a third, a whole cannonade. People began to shout from all sides, "An assault!"

Not knowing what to think, we rushed home. The firing did not cease. Near the house we saw Grandmother and Vera heading toward the trench. This trench seemed like such a fantastically ridiculous cover against such a shelling, a shelling which was shaking the very air, that I shouted to them to run back home. With the entire family and the neighbors, we rushed toward a little wing of the house in the middle of the garden. We closed the windows and doors and set up a genuine barricade of pillows, blankets, and everything we could lay our hands upon. We ourselves lay on the floor. The shelling grew more and more intense. It seemed that it was getting closer and closer. We had the impression that the battle was taking place on our very street. Old Grandmother kept crossing herself, thanking me for having taken her from the street. The noise reached such an intensity that it was difficult to know what was going on. Everything merged into one continuous roar.

Suddenly, everything grew hushed. This silence seemed especially weird, unearthly. Waiting a little while we opened the doors and then went out into the garden. It was quiet. The sun was already setting. The sky was the same clear, blue sky as in the morning. Only the air was smoky. It was so quiet that even the leaves on the trees were not rustling. Neither birds nor insects could be heard. Neither were people to be seen. It seemed as though a storm had struck and finished everything. We gathered courage and looked out on the street. At this second we heard the roar of an approaching tank. It was moving along our fence. On it were soldiers, in the open, weapons ready. Behind us, a fifteen-year-old girl, our neighbor's daughter, Milochka, burst out loudly and joyfully "Ours, ours returned, you see, they are coming back, they drove back the Germans." Behind the first tank came another, and another, a whole row. The setting sun illuminated the black sign of the iron cross. There could no longer be any doubt. The city had been occupied by the Germans.

Epilogue

I stopped this account at the moment when the German tanks entered Pyatigorsk. My notes continue far beyond this, however. With the arrival of the Germans, entirely new conditions and events followed one upon the other. New people and new impressions entered our lives. German rule in the Caucasus continued for five months. Many Russians were taken to Germany for forced labor; many fled to the Ukraine, further from the horrors of the front. Not having the possibility to leave earlier because of the lack of transport and money, we were able to leave flaming Pyatigorsk only through the kindness of a German officer, a pilot, who agreed to take us to the Ukraine. I have described in my diary our experiences in wandering through the war-ruined country up to that time that German occupation units mobilized us for labor in Germany. The trip through Poland along roads destroyed by partisans, blown-up trains, stations transformed into fortresses, ruined railroad lines, derailed trains—these are the pictures which flashed before us. Then came life in a camp in Poland near Lodz, dispatch to Germany for work in a war factory, almost two years in a camp for "East-workers," new encounters, new people, new sorrows, and some rare joys, called forth by the warm sympathies and understanding of some of these people, our recent enemies.

Nineteen forty-five, February and March, brought the last attempts of the Germans to defend their country. The pressure of the Allies, uninterrupted bombardments, the front line along the Rhine. We were on the opposite shore, behind us that very forest where German long-range artillery was concealed. Shells from both sides roared overhead. The work camp in which we lived was destroyed by incendiary bombs, burning to its very foundation. For three weeks we hid in a bunker bored into rock above the Rhine. On the 25th of March, American forces entered our little town. Soon they were replaced by Belgians, and at the beginning of July, after the partition of Germany into four zones, came the French and the establishment of the French occupation under which we lived for five years. I was immediately hired for work, at first in an officers' club, later in a cooperative, and finally by the Displaced Persons Administration.

The arrival in Frankfurt am Main from New York of the Russian writer on political and social problems and former Menshevik, Boris Nikolaevski, decided our future fate. He was collecting documents from witnesses of the Leningrad blockade. I went to Frankfurt and handed him my diaries. From then on, the Literary Fund in New York regularly supplied me with packages, the famous Care Packages which allowed us to live a poverty-free existence. Nikolaevski arranged for us the affidavits and visas for America. In Hamburg, on May 19, 1950, a huge military steamship gathered all those refugees accepted for immigration to the United States. We were among that number. We arrived in New York on May 31, 1950. Europe was far behind. We set foot on the soil of a new continent with new hopes and with a wish here, finally, to achieve rest and create that home which we had lost in Leningrad. I have written up an account of the events of our life up to this point. About the last part, our life in America, I am writing now.

Elena Skrjabina

Iowa City, Iowa
February 1971

List of Characters who survived the Siege and their destinations as of 1971

Skrjabina, Elena   Professor of Russian, University of Iowa.

Skrjabin, Sergey   heard that his wife and sons died in the Caucasus; married Irina Levitskaya; died in 1946.

Skrjabin, Dima   now a doctor in a large American city.

Skrjabin, Yuri   completed an American university; died in an accident at the age of 27.

Levitskaya, Irina   survived the war; married Sergey Skrjabin; now living in the former Skrjabin apartment in Leningrad.

Kurakina, Lubov Nikolayevna   evacuated, destination unknown.

Kholmyanskaya, Faina   evacuated, destination unknown.

Tanya   survived the war; married a French citizen; now living in Paris.

Lyalya (cousin)   survived the war; went back to Leningrad where she is now living.

Lyalya (sister-in-law)   survived the war; was a worker in a labor camp in Germany; returned to Russia and is again living in Pyatigorsk.

Aunt   evacuated to Siberia; died after returning to Leningrad at the end of the war.

Bolkhovskoi   died in Berlin in 1944, a victim of bombardment.

About the Author

Professor Elena Aleksandrovna Skrjabina was born in 1906 near Nizhni Novgorod (Gorki) and grew up in St. Petersburg (Leningrad) where her father was a member of the last Russian State Duma or parliament. Many important prerevolutionary figures were frequent visitors to their home, and as a small child she was exposed to many very important events. As an elementary school girl she witnessed the Russian revolution, the resultant Civil War and its attendant horrors.

In 1941, on the eve of the German attack, Elena Aleksandrovna was a young mother of two boys, pursuing graduate studies in French literature in Leningrad. She was happily married to Sergey Skrjabin, an engineer and a very close relative of the famous Russian composer of the same name. She had already, for a number of years prior to that, been keeping a diary; however, with the advent of the war, she began to record in her diary the events of those fateful times as she experienced them. This she did not only with the feeling and understanding of an actual participant, but with the great additional perception one would have expected from an outsider. Because of the tremendously difficult circumstances of those times, there were days when she was able to make only hasty and fragmentary notations in her diary. Thus it can be noted that at the beginning of the war, there was an eagerness to chronicle the events, and there were daily entries on June 22, 23, 24, 25, 26, etc. Then in October as the gloom occasioned by the rigors of the siege began to deepen, the entries became less frequent and shorter; October 12 is followed by October 18, which in turn is followed by October 26. By November, the full horrors of starvation were making themselves felt and on November 26 she was writing, "The death rate grows. They say as many as three thousand people die daily. . . . Sometimes you come across larger sleighs on which the corpses are piled high like firewood. . . . You observe death so closely that you stop reacting to it."

It is such simple, unadorned writing which makes this narrative so gripping. Wherever possible, I have tried in my translation to retain the original form and have attempted to keep it what it originally was, a day by day account of the greatest siege in history.

Many of the wartime notes were, of necessity, written on scraps of small paper until such time as she was able to again continue recording in notebooks. Years later, while in a German labor camp for *Ostarbeiter* ("workers from East Europe"), she went over these wartime notes and later published in Russian an account of the siege up to her arrival in Piatigorsk. This English account continues up to the arrival in the Caucasus of the Germans, which meant, of course, a complete change in her life and those with whom she was mostly concerned. In the meantime, she has continued working on her wartime notes and is finishing for possible publication a continuation of the diary to include her experiences through the German occupation, work camp in Germany, the coming of the Americans and French to Germany, etc.

Professor Skrjabina has been in the United States since 1950. Several years after her arrival in the United States, she taught Russian at the Air Force Language School in Syracuse, New York. While teaching in Syracuse, she entered the university there and received her American doctorate in French and comparative literature. Since 1960, she has been teaching at the University of Iowa where she is Professor of Russian. Among her articles and works, two books are perhaps worthy of special mention, *Les Faux Dieux*, a comparison of the Russian author Michail Zostchenko and the French author Marcel Aymé, published by Mercure de France, and a collection of Russian short stories for students of Russian, published by Harper and Row.

Afterword

In late August, 1939, as war clouds were darkening over Europe, the world was astounded by the news that the Soviet Union and Hitlerite Germany had signed a nonagression pact. This was all the more remarkable since throughout the 1930's none had railed more against the Bolshevik menace than had the Nazis; similarly, none had been more savage in their denunciation of the Nazi beasts than had the Soviets. Thus this Nazi-Soviet accord took the diplomatic world by surprise.

Hitler, now assured of Russian neutrality, felt free to press his claims against Poland despite Anglo-French insistence that they would support Poland if the latter were attacked. The new German Siegfried Line in the West could keep the French and British at bay while he finished with the Poles, and in the event of a somewhat protracted war, he could count on Russian supplies to avoid the worst stringencies of an Allied blockade. On September 1, 1939, Nazi forces swarmed into Poland. After seventeen days of fighting, the Poles were smashed and reeling. However, units were retreating to the east hoping to make a stand deeper in Poland. There the Germans would have to fight in worse terrain under worsening weather conditions, with more extended communication lines, while the Poles hoped to be supplied through Rumania. All the time, Britain would be strengthening her forces on Germany's Western Front. While it is doubtful that the Poles could have held out even in the east, the sudden invasion of Poland by the Russians on September 17 made further resistance virtually impossible. The Soviets and Germans shortly thereafter concluded a treaty of friendship and established a demarcation line between them; as a result of this and other agreements, the Soviets agreed to supply Germany with many of the raw materials necessary to carry on war.

In the spring of 1940, Nazi forces overran Denmark and Norway. In May they struck in the West. Holland fell in less than a week, Belgium in less than three, and even France, believed by many to have had the finest army in the world, fell within six weeks. Most of the British expeditionary forces fighting with the French had been able to get back to England; however, they had been forced to abandon virtually all their military equipment. Germany was thus master of the European mainland from the Russian Border to the English channel.

Of the three southern peninsulas of Europe, the Italian under Benito Mussolini was already in the war on Hitler's side. The Iberian was under the control of Francisco Franco, who was indebted to Mussolini and Hitler for aid he had received in the Spanish Civil War, and the Balkan seemed to be becoming drawn into the Nazi orbit as German influence, already paramount in Hungary, became more and more predominant in Rumania and Bulgaria.

Stalin, extremely worried by the tremendous German successes, feverishly tried to increase Russian military strength while at the same time doing everything possible not to offend Hitler. He had already taken advantage of German preoccupation in the West in June of 1940 to annex the Baltic republics of Lativa, Estonia, and Lithuania, and shortly thereafter he had forced Rumania to cede to him the province of Bessarabia and part of Bukovina, territories containing some four million persons. Rumania which had thereby already lost four million of her population of seventeen million to the USSR, now found herself faced with further demands by her neighbors. Under these conditions, Rumania announced that she had freely entered the sphere of the Axis (Nazi-Italian) powers and in October 1940, some German forces entered Rumania in order, as they told the Soviets, "to protect the oil fields." Regardless of how the Germans attempted to explain the presence of German troops in Rumania, the Soviets felt uneasy.

Meanwhile Hitler stood at the crossroads. He had been unable to wrest from the British uncontested air supremacy over the channel and the English coast. It was possible to attempt a cross-channel invasion without having uncontrolled air superiority. However, before such enormous risks, Hitler hesitated. What might happen if he should become bogged down in an English campaign and if the Russians would hold up supplies or, even worse, attack? He himself had invoked the law of the jungle and Soviets in their attack on Finland in the winter of 1939–40 had shown themselves bound by no moral scruples. Perhaps he could get the Russians to join him against the British if enough prospective booty were held out to them in the Middle East and India.

It was against this background, therefore, that

Russian Foreign Minister Molotov arrived in Berlin for talks in November 1940. Here the Germans tried to interest the Soviets in striking at the British lifeline in the Middle East. Molotov was more interested in gaining a predominant role for Russia in Rumania and the Balkans. The talks thus ended in failure and Hitler gave orders to continue drawing up plans for "Operation Barbarossa," the invasion of Russia, which was intended to begin in May 1941.

Hitler's decision was hastened by the knowledge that England's overseas dominions were sending more and more men and material to aid her. The United States was also beginning to send aid to England. Time, therefore, was not fighting for Germany. If he could gain a quick victory over Russia and avail himself of the latter's enormous raw materials, he would then be in an invincible position to either continue the war or to make peace on his terms.

Throughout the winter and spring of 1941, the Soviet leaders continued to fulfill all their trade and treaty obligations toward Germany. Hostile comment toward the latter not only did not appear in the Soviet press, but was kept out of the foreign Communist press, which continued to denounce World War II as an imperialist, capitalist war, and blame Britain for its continuance.

Meanwhile, Hitler's inept ally, Mussolini, had become bogged down in a campaign against Greece which he, disappointed with the meager gains Italy had so far acquired, and seeking military glory, had begun in October 1940. Hitler, unwilling to risk an invasion of Russia when his southern flank might be exposed to British planes and forces operating out of Greece, decided on a lightning campaign in the

Balkans in April 1941. Because of this campaign, it was not until late June, rather than May, that his forces were in position for an attack on the Soviet Union.

Warnings that the Germans were preparing to attack had come to the Soviet leader from a number of sources including even Winston Churchill. Stalin had dismissed these warnings as provocations; however, he was worried and did greatly strengthen Soviet forces in the front areas and did everything possible to keep from provoking a German attack.

The German attack, coming as it did on June 21, 1941, apparently caught the Soviet leaders by complete surprise. The Russian civilian population, while it had always felt that there was something unnatural about the friendship pact with Germany, had absolutely no inkling that war was imminent. The reactions of quite a significant cross section of Russians are brought out in this diary.

In the opening stages of the war the Germans advanced with great speed, Army Group North heading for Leningrad something like five hundred miles from the German-Soviet border, while the other two army groups headed for Moscow and the Ukraine respectively. During these opening battles Russian resistance was spotty, extremely stubborn resistance by some units, lack of will to fight by others. Within two days, Vilna had fallen; within two weeks, Riga. More than six hundred thousand Russian prisoners were taken in the encirclement at Bialystok near the frontier; about the same number were taken in the battle of Vyazma, and again as many in the battle for Kiev which the Germans took on September 19, 1941. Again this diary provides a strong insight into the type of spirit prevailing among many Russians in Leningrad at that time. In certain areas of White Russia and the Ukraine, the Germans were even greeted as liberators by significant segments of the population, for they had suffered grievously under the Stalinization of the preceding years. There were many Russians who did not care to fight for Stalin and the type of Communism they had experienced.

However, Hitler was revealing that he had no intention of confining this operation to a battle to bring down Communism. This was being turned into a battle against the Slavs, for living room in the East and huge estates to reward certain Nazi paladins. The Nazi leader, drunk with previous successes, felt no necessity to honor the normal rules of warfare and word of Nazi excesses drifted back to the Russians. But meanwhile the Russians were rallying. Stalin's appeal to Russian national feeling was bearing fruit, and the Nazi advance on the Leningrad and Moscow fronts was slowed down considerably in the fall of 1941, as Leningrad, now cut off from the rest of the country, entered its period of martyrdom. Those women, children, and other dependents who had not already abandoned the city before the Germans cut the roads began to starve. German offensive operations were halted and the Russians began a number of small counter attacks. Lake Ladoga froze and a very tenuous evacuation and supply route across the frozen lake was opened up. It was across this lake that Professor Skrjabina and thousands of emaciated Leningraders were evacuated during that first horrible winter of war.

With the end of winter and the advent of better weather the Germans in 1942 began a new push into southern Russia; one army swept to the Volga at

Stalingrad, while other forces moved into the Caucasus taking, among other places, Pyatigorsk, to which Professor Skrjabina had evacuated. It is with the coming of the Germans into the Caucasus, the furthest German penetration into Russia, that this account ends. The war continued another three bitter years, with the Germans being pushed back, back, and then back again, until the final Götterdämmerung in the smoking ruins of gutted Berlin in 1945.

I first became acquainted with Elena Skrjabina in 1963 while attending a Modern Language Teachers' convention where she delivered a paper on the Russian social humorist, Michail Zostchenko. During the next several years, I met Mme. Skrjabina at several other conferences. Thus when a colleague informed me that her *Diary of the Siege of Leningrad* had been published in Russian, I was interested in seeing it. I remember glancing at it rather casually, intending more or less to get a general idea of its contents rather than actually reading it through. Then as I skimmed through the first several pages, my attention was drawn to such a degree that I had to read it to the end before I could put it down.

Although I had specialized in Russian history and although I had quite a bit of contact with Russians, it was not until I had read that diary that I had had any real conception of what Leningrad and the Leningraders had really endured during the war. Most of my information had come from such sources as the *Encyclopedia Britannica* which states:

During World War II from mid-August 1941, Leningrad was a besieged city with the Finns to the north and the Germans to the south. Communication with the rest of the country was possible only in the winter months across the frozen Ladoga sea. The city was heavily damaged by German artillery fire and air-bombing. But in spite of the great shortage of supplies and food, the Soviet armed forces worked to supply material for the front. After a 900 day siege Leningrad was freed from the blockage at the end of January 1944. During the fighting 3,174 buildings were burned to the ground and 7,143 damaged by shells and bombs. By 1950 the city's reconstruction was basically completed. (Vol. 23, pp. 791–92.)

and the *Bol'shaya Sovetskaya Entsiklopediya* which states:

During the period of the Great Fatherland War the Leningrad party organization fulfilled the instructions of the Central Committee of the Party. In the shortest time possible, it put industry on a war footing. . . . In spite of the difficult conditions of the blockade, industry continued to turn out arms and shells for the Soviet army and the fleet. The Soviet government displayed a continual care about Leningrad. The whole Soviet nation gave aid to Leningrad which was surrounded in 1941. In spite of food shortages and deprivations connected with the blockade, uninterrupted aerial and artillery bombardment, the shining defenders of Leningrad repulsed all attacks of the enemy who were trying to take over the city. From January 17 to January 27, 1944, Leningrad was completely liberated. (Vol. 24, p. 524.)

It is doubtful that anyone having read Mme. Skrjabina's account can be satisfied with the above descriptions of the siege. However, in addition to its historical value for me, I found this account so gripping and so moving that I immediately contacted Mme. Skrjabina about the possibility of translating it into English.

Afterword

I have tried insofar as possible to retain the original short, clear, concise phrasing; the intention is to keep the account what it originally was, a day-by-day description of the greatest and, because of its scope, the most horrible siege in world history. There has been nothing added to the original account.

Norman Luxenburg

Iowa City, Iowa
February 1971

Index of Names and Places

It is common Russian usage to use only first names followed by the father's first name in referring to or in addressing someone. Thus the common way of referring to Elena Skrjabina would be Elena Aleksandrovna, after her father's name, Aleksandr. A boy, Boris, whose father's name is Aleksandr would be called Boris Aleksandrovich.

In general, I have followed the Library of Congress system of transliteration. However, for easier pronunciation, I have used "ya" and "ye" instead of "ia" and "ie," thus names will be written Levitskaya instead of Levitskaia, etc. I have also shortened Russian endings to "ski" instead of "skii" as in Kholmyanski [tr.].

INDEX OF NAMES

Index of Names

INDEX OF PLACES